# LA PARILLA

# LA PARILLA

## the mexican grill

by Reed Hearon

Photographs by Laurie Smith

CHRONICLE BOOKS

SAN FRANCISCO

Text copyright © 1996 by Reed Hearon
Photographs copyright © 1996 by Laurie Smith

Library of Congress Cataloging-in-Publication Data available.

ISBN 0-8118-1034-8

Printed in Hong Kong

Designed by Jim Christie

Distributed in Canada by Raincoast Books
8680 Cambie Street
Vancouver, B.C. V6P 6M9

10 9 8 7 6 5 4 3 2 1

Chronicle Books
275 Fifth Street
San Francisco, CA 94103

To Louise and the staff at Café Marimba for helping me to realize a dream, and to my friends Soledad, Henry, Rosa, and others in Mexico for providing the guidance and courage to pursue that dream. And to Jackie, whom we all miss.

Acknowledgments

Thank you, Tim, for your help in writing this book. Thanks also to Penni and Bill for making it happen in time and, most of all, for making it whole, complete, and real—which it otherwise never would have been. Thanks to Fred for believing in me and helping in so many ways. And to Christy and all the crew at LuLu for putting up with my absences and for being examples of what it means to be dedicated. To Shelby and Bob, thanks for being there.

# contents

# introduction

Picture nightfall on the coast of Mexico. A pile of mesquite branches is gathered and a fire is lit. A glistening red snapper, caught moments before, is quickly cleaned and smeared with a paste of citrus and spices. It sizzles briefly as it is laid across the grill.

The sight, sound, and smell of a piece of spicy fish hitting a hot grill conjure up a host of primitive memories. Some accident involving fire probably gave humans their first taste of cooked food. Ever since, fire has been the focus of food preparation and the social activity surrounding it. Even today, in our age of microwaves and frozen food, the backyard grill rekindles a primitive memory of communal feasting.

From the coast of Quintana Roo to the cattle country of Northern Mexico, the grill defines the celebration of life that is Mexican cooking. This is real food. Earthy. Healthful. Full of flavor. Fun—and easy—to cook and eat.

I will begin this exploration of the Mexican grill with brief descriptions of typical ingredients, techniques, and equipment. If, in a specific recipe, you find something unfamiliar, please refer back to this section for a full explanation. I will then turn to cooking with *recados*, one of four essential building blocks of the Mexican grill. *Recados* are spice mixtures from the Yucatán peninsula and are little known outside of Mexico. Used for seasoning meats, fish, and poultry for the grill, they can usually be assembled in a few minutes and may be made ahead of time.

Salsas are the second crucial building block of the Mexican grill. Colorful, spicy, and always fun, salsas enliven all types of food. Grilled foods seem to demand the picante, cleansing edge that they give. Using techniques from pre-conquest Mexico, we will make more than a dozen salsas, each a bundle of unexpected flavor.

Fresh, soft tortillas form the third building block, bringing together seasoned meat and salsa. Tortillas are indispensable to the Mexican grill. If you've ever seen a four-year-old clutching a piece of meat wrapped in a tortilla, you can appreciate that nothing satisfies quite like a tortilla. And corn, not flour, tortillas are the whole-grain foundation of the Mexican grill.

Finally, we need a fire to grill over. You can grill successfully over gas or charcoal briquettes, or even simulate a grill with a hot iron skillet, but nothing tastes of Mexico like mesquite. Fortunately, mesquite charcoal (not briquettes) is widely available across the United States. I will discuss fires, grills, and most important, what to grill and how to grill it.

Although some of the ingredients sound strange (like epazote) and some of the cooking techniques seem exotic (grilled goat cheese in banana leaves or salmon wrapped in corn husks), the pleasure of the Mexican grill is that it is so simple. It is about a few ingredients, creatively prepared and combined to maximize flavor, then cooked over a fire, and served with spicy, contrasting salsas. You will need to seek out a supply of chiles, and I have given some sources in the next chapter. After that, all you need is a grocery store and a few minutes to savor the simple pleasure of cooking over a fire the Mexican way.

# grilling the mexican way

way

ingredients

techniques

equipment

# ingredients

**Achiote paste:** This moist, brick-colored seasoning paste is available in most Mexican and Latin American food markets. It is a blend of the iodiney seeds of the annatto tree, citrus juices, vinegar plus other spices. The flavor will vary with brand and freshness, so be sure to taste it before using. It keeps almost indefinitely, tightly covered, at room temperature.

**Ancho chile powder:** Made from ground ancho chiles, the powder can be found in most good Mexican groceries. To make your own, fry ancho chiles in 1 tablespoon vegetable oil over medium-high heat until puffed and browned, 5 to 10 seconds. Drain well on paper towels. Grind into a powder in a blender or food processor.

**Annatto seeds:** These are the hard red seeds of the annatto tree, native to the tropics. They are softened by soaking in hot water for 2 hours before grinding for use (see page 20 for specifics). Annatto seeds tint foods a bright yellow and are familiar to you as the dye used to color Cheddar cheese orange and butter yellow.

**Avocado leaves:** The heady anise aroma that characterizes much of Oaxacan cookery comes from the avocado leaf. At Café Marimba, we use the particularly pungent variety grown in Southern Mexico. The dried leaves can be purchased in Mexico or through my restaurant, Café Marimba (see Sources). The leaves often have galls on the undersides; these have a concentrated flavor and are edible. To prepare the leaves, toast them in a dry skillet over medium heat (or, using tongs, hold them over an open flame) until browned and fragrant, about 10 seconds. Then grind, if the recipe calls for grinding. Toast only as many leaves as you will use at one time.

**Banana leaves:** One of the first cooking vessels available to man was the leaf. Foods wrapped and cooked in banana leaves pick up the oily, anise-like aroma characteristic of bananas. Toasting them briefly over an open flame releases their fragrance. The leaves are about 16 inches wide and 4 to 5 feet long. They are available, packed in plastic pouches, in the frozen-food sections of some Asian, Latin American, and Mexican markets.

**Chiles:** More than thirty different varieties of chiles have been identified, with literally hundreds of subtypes. Chiles, like wine grapes, reflect the soil, climate, and growing conditions where they were cultivated. Connoisseurs will pay high prices for chiles grown in certain regions or dried under special conditions. As you familiarize yourself with chiles, you will come to understand why. Each chile brings much more than heat to a dish. Smoky, sweet, sharp, astringent—every variety has a unique flavor. The most important things to know are whether the chile is fresh or dried and how hot it is. When using the recipes

in this book, avoid trying to modulate heat by varying the quantity of a particular chile. Heat is merely one of many flavor components. Varying the amount of a given chile in a dish may throw it out of balance. If you don't like hot food, don't use less of a chile; instead make a dish that uses a different chile. Below, I have described briefly the chiles I believe most essential. Later on, I have listed some mail-order suppliers.

**Fresh chiles:**

**Anaheim:** This long, green chile is the most widely grown mild chile. Pale green and 5 to 7 inches long, it can be a bit anemic in flavor, but is much improved by roasting, particularly over a wood fire.

**Habanero:** This small, round chile is purported to be the hottest in the world. It is a different species than all other chiles commonly eaten in this country. Aside from its remarkable heat, it has an elusive floral-citrusy flavor that makes it highly prized as a component to many salsas. This chile is still rare in the United States. If you see it, buy some and see what all the fuss is about. It is available in green, yellow, and orange, reflecting different degrees of ripeness.

**Jalapeño:** This is probably the most familiar and popular hot chile. Ranging from two to three inches in length, with a fat shape and dark, shiny green skin, the fresh jalapeño can be eaten raw or roasted. It is also widely available pickled (look for the brands packed in Mexico). A variety of jalapeño, the chipotle, is dried by slowly smoking it over peat. It adds a wonderful smoky savor to soups and salsas. When using jalapeños, check to see whether the recipe calls for seeds. The seeds themselves have a distinct, sharp flavor that is vital to some dishes.

**New Mexico:** The king of the U.S. canning industry, this long, green chile can vary from insipid to intensely flavored and fire-hot, depending on where it is grown. The best come from around Chimayo, but are unavailable outside of the immediate area. If you see these chiles fresh in the store, buy some, roast them over a mesquite fire, and enjoy a taste of New Mexico.

**Poblano:** This is the preferred chile of chiles rellenos—big (about 5 inches long) and heart-shaped, dark green, meaty, and mildly spicy. Poblanos are wonderful roasted and, if you are careful and do not overly blacken the skin, you do not have to peel them. Just pull off the stem, and with it will come the seed core. Milder Anaheims are the best substitute. The poblano, especially in California, is often incorrectly labeled a pasilla chile. Ancho chiles are dried poblanos.

**Serrano:** This small, light-green chile is skinny and pointed, about 2 inches long. It has a bright, clean heat and flavor, and can be significantly hotter than the jalapeño. Always use the seeds. They are vital to the serrano's flavor.

**Dried chiles:**

**Ancho:** The ancho is the dried version of the red, ripe poblano, and is perhaps the most widely used dried chile in Mexico. About 5 inches long, reddish-brown, and very wrinkled, it has a mildly spicy, sweet, plummy, raisiny flavor that is delicious in a wide range of salsas, *recados*, and moles. Look for soft, flexible chiles that smell fresh, not musty.

**Árbol:** Usually the dried version of the ripe serrano, the skinny, reddish-brown *chile de árbol* varies from 1 to 3 inches long. It is hot but also has a pleasant nutty, rich flavor when toasted. Often toasted and used whole in soups or stews, when crushed or ground these chiles can pack a real wallop. These are widely available and often sold whole as "red chiles."

**Chipotle:** This is the dried, ripe version of a particular type of jalapeño and one of my favorite chiles. It is slowly cured over peat fires, giving it a smoky, rich flavor. Ranging from 3 to 4 inches long and dusty brown, chipotles are perhaps better known in the canned condiment, *chipotle en adobo* (chiles simmered in adobo sauce). This is very hot! Those who can stand the heat will appreciate the wonderful rich flavor. Seek out the dried chipotle in Mexican and Latin American markets or through mail order.

**Guajillo:** This is the dried version of the Mexican (unhybridized) version of the New Mexico–type red chile. It is about 4 inches long, reddish-brown, and smooth-skinned. Its medium heat and nutty flavor make it a versatile chile for salsas and moles. Use it in conjunction with chipotles or moritas for a complex layering of flavor and heat.

**Morita:** This chile is like the smaller brother of the chipotle. It, too, is a smoked, dried chile made from a small jalapeño grown in the state of Michoacán. It is very hot, but not as hot as the chipotle and, also like the chipotle, is often sold canned as *chipotle en adobo*. It is a small chile, about 1½ inches long and reddish. It is widely used in Veracruz.

**Pasilla:** This is a blackish chile, 5 to 8 inches long with a deep cocoalike flavor. Unfortunately, the name pasilla is used in parts of the United States to refer not to a dried chile but instead to the fresh poblano.

**Dried Mexican oregano:** Mexican oregano has a flavor distinct from Greek oregano. Greek oregano tastes like pizza, while Mexican oregano tastes like Mexican food. Do not substitute one for the other. It is easily found in Mexican and Latin American markets. Mexican oregano develops its full flavor when toasted in a dry skillet until fragrant.

**Epazote:** On its own, epazote, a deep green herb with serrated leaves, has a strange medicinal smell, almost like kerosene. It is essential in a wide range of dishes, including a large number of Veracruz specialties, as well as black beans. The herb should always be used fresh. The flavor of the dried version bears no resemblance to the fresh. Epazote is becoming more widely available, especially in Southern California and Texas. See Sources for mail-order plant suppliers.

**Hierba santa/Hoja santa:** *Hierba* means "herb" and *hoja* means "leaf." This large, heart-shaped leaf adds an incomparable exotic aroma hinting of anise, camphor, or even sassafras to Oaxacan and Veracruzano dishes. It is becoming more widely available in the United States but is still difficult to find. It is best when fresh, but the dried herb makes a good substitute. Refresh the dried herb before using by soaking in warm water a few minutes. Squeeze out excess water before proceeding with the recipe. See Sources for mail-order suppliers.

**Nopales:** The flat, dark-green "leaf" or paddle of the nopal cactus, also known as the prickly pear cactus, is widely eaten in Mexico. It has a pleasant, sappy, almost green-bean flavor. The only problem is that the nopal comes with small needles that will stick in your hands as you clean the leaves. In Mexico, seemingly every market sells neat little bags of already cleaned, whole nopal paddles. Unfortunately, here you must usually clean them yourself. But don't fear. Put on an old pair of gardening gloves, take a small paring knife, and cut off each of the little bumps that contain the needles. Fresh, whole nopales are fairly widely available in supermarkets throughout the Southwest.

**Olive oil:** When I call for olive oil in Mexican cooking, I am not thinking of the finely flavored extra-virgin olive oils of Italy or France, but of the lighter-tasting, more neutral pure oils. Their more delicate flavor harmonizes better with Mexican fare.

**Pineapple vinegar:** Mexico grows incredible amounts of pineapple, so it is readily available for making vinegar stock. Pineapple vinegar is used frequently in Mexican cooking, but, to my knowledge, it is not available in the United States. A good substitute is apple cider vinegar. You might experiment with making your own pineapple vinegar by combining 1 cup fresh pineapple purée, a pinch of ground allspice, 1 tablespoon brown sugar or Mexican sugar (unrefined dark brown sugar sold in cone-shaped molds), and 6 cups white wine vinegar (6 percent acidity) in a large nonreactive saucepan. Bring to a simmer, turn off the heat, and let steep overnight. Strain into a clean glass jar with a nonmetallic lid and store at room temperature. This makes about 6 cups.

**Pork lard:** The best pork lard has a browned pork flavor. The lard that is commercially available in supermarkets is so refined it has little flavor left. Seek out freshly rendered pork lard in Mexican and Chinese markets. Or flavor packaged pork lard by adding a few tablespoons bacon drippings. You can also substitute olive oil, but you will lose the authentic flavor.

**Queso fresco:** Queso fresco is about as simple as cheese can get: the strained, salted curds of cow's milk. It is a fresh cheese with a bit of a tang. I find it is similar to feta, although good-quality fetas, being made from sheep's milk, have a different flavor. Finding a proper substitute depends on its use in the recipe. Look for queso fresco in Mexican groceries.

**Tamarind:** The citric, sweet-sour flavor of tamarind goes well with chiles. Tamarind, a seedpod native to Asia but widely grown in Mexico, is used most often in beverages. It is one of the flavorings in cola drinks, as well as in Worcestershire sauce. Only the pulp that clings to the seeds under the brittle pod is commonly used. Pods and prepared pulp are easily found in Latin American and Asian groceries. When you make the pulp yourself, it tastes much fresher than the prepared kind. To make fresh tamarind pulp, put 2½ cups shelled tamarind pods in a small saucepan and add just enough water to cover. Cover with a lid, bring to a boil over medium heat, and simmer gently until the pulp loosens and falls off the seeds, about 30 minutes. Stir frequently to speed the process. Add more water if the mixture becomes too thick. Strain through a medium sieve, pushing hard with the back of a spoon to extract as much paste as possible. You should have about 1½ cups. If not, add a little more water, bring back to a boil, and strain again to remove more pulp.

**Tortillas:** Virtually every recipe in this book ends with the instruction, "Serve with plenty of fresh, hot tortillas." The corn tortilla plays a fundamental role in Mexican food, even more so than bread does in country French food. It not only finds a central place in every meal, but it also defines dishes like quesadillas, tacos, enchiladas, and, in one form or another, all of those items that Mexicans call *antojitos* and most of the rest of us think of as Mexican food.

Just as connoisseurs of great pasta or bread insist on an artisanal product, Mexicans seek out the best tortillas. In Oaxaca there are three different sizes, ranging from small white blonditas to giant, wafer-thin *tlayudas*. The finest of these are tortillas *a mano*, handmade tortillas.

Tortillas in Mexico almost always mean corn tortillas. Flour tortillas are a relatively recent import from the United States, their popularity driven by the low cost of inferior grades of flour dumped into border markets and by their ability to keep and ship well. While flour tortillas can be delicious, they are nutritionally suspect and do not complement the flavor of most Mexican food. I think of most flour tortillas in the same way I think of commercial presliced white breads—convenient but not much else.

Making your own corn tortillas at home is as easy as going to a tortilla factory (every medium-sized U.S. city now seems to have one) and buying fresh *masa para tortillas* and pressing it out between two sheets of waxed paper with a small rolling pin or a hand tortilla press. The tortillas are then cooked dry on a hot griddle or frying pan until they brown on both sides and puff slightly.

But if making your own tortillas is not in the picture, don't despair. Commercial corn tortillas can be very good. Look for the whitest ones (which indicate less lime used in processing the corn and, hence, a more delicate flavor), and make sure that they are fresh. Buy tortillas, just as you would bread, from a source that sells a lot of them. They should be very soft and flexible in their plastic bags. If you are lucky, you will see telltale beads of water in the bags, indicating steam from the cooling tortillas. They may even be warm. And, just as you would bread, they are best used the day they are made.

To reheat tortillas, you need an intense source of dry heat. The best way is on a griddle or iron skillet preheated until very hot over medium-high heat. The tortillas should be individually warmed on each side until they color slightly. As they are warmed, stack them and wrap in a clean, dry cotton towel. Keep them covered until you are ready to use them. If you wish, the towel may be wrapped in foil and kept in a 200°F oven for up to an hour to keep the tortillas warm. Tortillas may also be heated directly on the grates of a grill. The procedure is the same and they pick up a nice smoky flavor, although they are prone to burning.

Make eating tortillas a habit. They are low in calories, high in fiber, and delicious with all sorts of food. Just remember, serve them hot and as fresh as possible.

# techniques

After the first accidental falling of food into the fire and the first necessary burned tongue came the discovery that food cooked in fire tasted good. Then came the slow evolution of cooking utensils. At first, food was probably simply thrown into the fire. Then perhaps it was suspended above the fire on a green stick. Eventually, people must have realized that the stones around and in the fire got very hot. These stones became the first grills and griddles. Later, clay was used to form pots and *comals* for cooking. With the introduction of iron to Mexico by the Spaniards, the grill as we know it arrived in the New World. A magical change it was.

Mastering the Mexican approach to grilling is a matter of understanding a few basics. Once those basics are mastered, anyone can turn out delicious grilled foods. Beyond the fundamentals lie hundreds of tricks that come to the practitioner over time. I will try to highlight these throughout this book as I discuss techniques for grilling different foods. But first the basics:

**What to grill:** Almost any kind of meat, fish, poultry, game, or vegetable can be grilled. For meat the easiest items to grill are tender, naturally flavorful cuts. These top cuts include steaks, chops, filleted fish, boneless poultry, and other relatively thin, easy-to-eat foods. They do tend to be expensive and can be somewhat monotonous after awhile. As a chef, I find whole fish, roasts, lamb shanks, bone-in poultry, and the like much more interesting to grill and eat. Foods cooked on the bone shrink less and tend to have more flavor. While they are more challenging to cook, they are worth the trouble and tend to be much less expensive. Many Mexican grill techniques are geared toward less tender foods that require long, slow cooking.

**Using *recados* and salsas for flavor:** The Mexican grill relies on two key methods of flavoring foods. One, the *recado*, is used to season food before it is cooked. Sometimes, foods need to be marinated for hours or even overnight before grilling. Do not stint on marinating times given in the recipes; the times reflect how long it will take for the *recado* to reach the interior of the food to season and tenderize fully and to help maintain moisture. When salt is listed as an ingredient, it is usually not only there to add flavor but also to raise the moisture level chemically in the food. If you alter the level of salt in some of the recipes, it may result in a dish that is dry as well as bland.

The second method of flavoring is the salsa. Salsas are used as an accompaniment to grilled foods. Whereas *recados* tend to heighten the natural flavor of the foods being grilled, salsas provide contrast or counterpoint—setting the natural flavors in relief. Salsas rely in part on chiles to provide both flavor and heat. While it is possible to reduce the heat of a salsa by reducing the number of chiles, you also reduce the very flavor of the mixture itself. Instead of using fewer chiles, try making a different salsa based on a milder chile.

**Grilling poultry:** The best analogy I can give for properly grilling poultry is to cook the skin like bacon. You want to render the fat and then let the skin brown and crisp. To do this and have meat that is cooked through and still very moist, grill over a slow fire. Begin grilling the poultry skin-side down and placed on the grill to one side of the fire, not directly over it. Move the pieces, but do not turn, until the fat renders and the skin begins to brown. Turn them, skin-side up, if the skin is browning too fast. You can also cover the grill, leaving it open a crack, to slow the cooking. Turn poultry on the horizontal plane as well, first one side toward the fire, then the other side. Once the skin has begun to brown, turn the poultry over and finish cooking on the other side. Turn skin-side down for the last few minutes to recrisp the skin.

**Toasting and grinding herbs and spices such as cumin and Mexican oregano:** Toasting herbs and spices takes only a minute or two and improves their flavor appreciably. It also adds another layer of complexity to their taste. Often a recipe calls for a very small amount of a spice or herb. Buy spices and herbs in small amounts in stores that sell them in bulk and have a good turnover rate. This way you can be sure they are fresh and full of flavor. You might even want to store whole spices in the freezer if you will not be using them within a relatively short period of time.

My advice is to toast and grind a tablespoon or so once a week so you will have it on hand. Heat the spice or herb in a small, heavy, dry skillet over medium heat. Cook just until fragrant and beginning to brown, probably less than 2 minutes. Immediately pour into a small bowl to let cool. Grind in a spice mill and transfer to a small, tightly sealed jar.

**Pan-roasting white onions, garlic, tomatoes, tomatillos, sweet peppers, and fresh and dried chiles:** Ingredients are simply placed on a dry, clean, hot *comal* or grill. This pan-roasting adds a toasty, nutty flavor and is the secret to many of the complex flavors in *recados* and salsas. This method dates from before the introduction of most cooking fats by the Spaniards. The only fats native to Mexico were pumpkin seed oil and armadillo fat, neither in quantities sufficient for sautéing and frying as we know it. Toasting foods on a *comal*, or flat metal or earthenware griddle, is a method still in wide use today. Any flat, heavy pan can be substituted. Heat it over low or medium-low heat and arrange the vegetables on it without any added fats or oils. Cook carefully so they brown slowly but do not blacken or burn. Turn the vegetables occasionally to ensure that they cook evenly on all sides. When done, the vegetables will often "boil"; bubbles of water will be visible breaking through to the surface. At this point, the cell structure has broken down and the water within the cells is boiling, which means that the vegetables will be soft throughout.

To pan-roast white onions, peel them and cut horizontally into ½-inch-thick slices. Separate garlic heads into cloves but do not peel until after cooking. Onions and garlic will take 10 to 20 minutes to roast. Tomatoes and tomatillos may take a little longer, depending on their size. Leave tomatoes and tomatillos whole and unpeeled. Remove the husks of tomatillos. The tomato and tomatillo skins will blister—if you are careful they will not blacken, but turn a deep brown where they touch the griddle. The same is true of sweet peppers and fresh chiles that are pan-roasted whole. Tomatoes, tomatillos, sweet peppers, and fresh chiles are usually not peeled after pan-roasting, unless the skin is tough or burned—so try not to burn them. Pull off the stems and remove the seed cores (do not seed the peppers and chiles unless directed in a recipe) after they are pan-roasted. Dried chiles can also be pan-roasted. Press them lightly against the griddle with a spatula; they will take only a few seconds to puff and turn fragrant.

**Frying dried chiles:** This is a modern technique, since the routine use of fat in cooking only arrived with the Spanish. Frying dried chiles in oil toasts them, and the bit of added oil helps carry their nutty flavor to the dish in which they are used. The resulting chile flavor is slightly hotter than it would be if the pepper were toasted on a *comal* because capsicum (the compound responsible for chiles' hot flavor) dissolves in oil. Fry the dried chiles in hot corn oil for 5 to 10 seconds, just until they puff and have browned. Do not let them burn or they will taste bitter. It is usually unnecessary to drain the peppers on paper towels; instead just shake off the excess oil. After frying, the chiles are often soaked in boiling water until soft, about 20 minutes.

**Seeding and deveining dried chiles:** Seeding and deveining chiles makes them less hot. It also changes their flavor. It is not always necessary to remove seeds and stems, but if the recipe calls for it, begin by pulling off and discarding the stems. Break the chiles open, shake out the seeds, then pull off the veins. The chiles are now ready to be soaked, toasted, fried, or ground, depending on the recipe.

**Handling and preparing fresh sweet peppers and chiles:** If you have sensitive skin, wear plastic or rubber gloves when handling fresh hot chiles, as their natural oils can irritate and burn. Always wash your hands well immediately after you have finished working with chiles, and never touch sensitive parts of your body, such as lips and eyes, until you have done so.

Sometimes a recipe's instructions will say to remove the seed core, which means to pull off the stem. The fat central seed core will come with it. Do not then remove the rest of the seeds, but slice or dice the chile as the recipe indicates. When the recipe says to seed the pepper or chile, pull off the stem and remove the seed core, then cut in half and cut out the white veins and shake out any remaining seeds.

**Peeling fresh sweet peppers and chiles:** I don't do this often, but sometimes the skin, especially that of bell peppers, can be tough. In that case, pull off the stem and remove the seed cores. Cut the peppers in pieces, lengthwise, between the lobes. Cut out the veins, shake out the remaining seeds, and then use a sharp, swivel-bladed vegetable peeler to shave off the outer skin of the pepper.

I like another technique that lessens the watery flavor and intensifies the color of sweet peppers that are to be used raw in salads and salsas. After cleaning them, lay the pieces on a counter, skin side down, and press as flat as possible. Then, with a sharp paring knife, fillet the pepper pieces, cutting off all the inside ridges and veins to leave only the fattest, reddest flesh.

**Roasting sweet peppers and chiles:** Choose peppers and chiles with thick flesh. Roast them over an open flame—on the grill, in the fireplace, under the broiler, or over a gas burner. Turn the peppers so they char evenly. Put them in a bowl, uncovered, and let steam several minutes, until cool enough to handle. Pull off the stems and seed cores. Peel off the skin if it is tough and/or burned; otherwise, don't bother. Cut out the veins and remove the seeds if you wish or if the recipe calls for this step.

# equipment

**Brushes:** Get a long-handled stiff wire brush for cleaning the grill after each use and after lighting a fresh fire.

**Grills:** There is a wide range of grills available. One of the best I have used was made from a 55-gallon drum cut in half with a grate made of thick metal rods. Professional kitchens have sturdy grills that also use heavy—frequently cast iron—grill grates. All the recipes for this book were tested using a Weber kettle-type grill. This grill works well and can be improved by using a cast-iron grate insert sold at some specialty retailers.

The chief things to look for in a grill are sufficient space between the fire and the grate (10 inches is about right); a lid that can be put over the grill to slow an overly hot fire and create a smoky environment; a hinged grate for ease in adding more fuel to the fire; cast-iron grill grates, which preheat and cook more evenly, and are less prone to stick; and good airflow to the fire.

**Fuel for grilling:** While the food to be grilled and the way it is seasoned both help determine the final flavor, the fuel used is just as important in determining the end result. The most typical fuel used in Mexico is mesquite, either in the form of dry hardwood or charcoal (but not charcoal briquettes). Mesquite charcoal is convenient, if a little messy, and gives a superior effect. It may be hard to find in some areas, however.

I prefer building a fire of natural hardwood to using briquettes. Briquettes can give a chemical flavor to food and do not burn hot enough to sear foods properly. Natural hardwoods such as oak, almond, mesquite, and apple burn longer and hotter and give a wonderful true wood flavor to grilled foods. They have two small drawbacks that make them less convenient than briquettes: They are time-consuming to light and burn down to a proper level, and the pieces tend to be overly large for most home grills. In many areas, you can buy hardwood chunks (not the smaller chips) in small bags. These work great by themselves as a fuel for home grilling. Gas grills are convenient and easy to use, but flavor is sacrificed.

**Kitchen towels:** Better than gloves, a clean, dry, thick kitchen towel is both pot holder and wipe.

**Molcajete:** A lava-rock mortar and pestle *(tejolote)* are widely used in Mexico for making salsas. Not only is such a mortar the best tool for making guacamole and many salsas, but it also makes a handsome serving dish. And it is easier to clean than a food processor.

**Spatula:** A sturdy, professional metal spatula with a wooden handle is best for turning difficult-to-handle foods.

**Spice mill:** The flavor given by freshly ground herbs and spices is not to be underestimated. It is one of the simplest, easiest ways for your home cooking to take a leap forward in quality. Buy a pepper mill for freshly ground pepper and an inexpensive electric coffee mill to devote to spices. Often in this book we use a chipotle rub and a garlic rub both as a marinade and a last-minute seasoning alternative to salt. If they have clumped up, you can use your spice mill to grind the rubs just before use so that they can be sprinkled evenly over the food. You will find yourself using your spice mill often—for cumin seeds, for dried Mexican oregano, for dried chiles. Wipe the spice mill out with a paper towel between uses. You can even use it for grinding coffee beans if you are careful about cleaning it, although it can be a rough morning if you forget.

**Spray bottle with water:** This is useful for putting out the little flare-ups that come from a fire that is too hot or food that is too close to the fire. Or use a cold beer if you happen to have one handy.

**Tongs:** For me, long-handled, professional-style tongs are essential to successful grilling. Tongs are inexpensive and permit you to pick up, move, and turn food easily without tearing or piercing it. If you are like me and tend to leave them here and there on your trips from kitchen to barbecue and back, you might want to get several pairs.

recados

# One of the keys

to the bright flavors of the Mexican grill is the family of seasoning mixtures used on meats, fish, poultry, and vegetables before they are grilled. These little-known seasonings stem, for the most part, from Yucatán cooking and are called *recados*, meaning "complements." Part marinade, part spice mix, *recados* do indeed complement the flavors of the foods they season, transforming them from raw ingredient to finished dish.

Complex layers of flavor come from individually roasting or cooking each ingredient. The separate ingredients are then mixed together to create a single flavor—typically in a stone-wheeled grinder or in home kitchens in a blender, food processor, or, more traditionally, in a *molcajete*. Sometimes, the resulting paste is cooked again to add yet another, deeper flavor.

*Recados* have their counterparts in other cuisines: France has its *quatre épices* and *herbes de Provence*, India its *garam masala*, China its five-spice powder. Like those spice mixes, *recados* are often added to soups, stews, and braises, or used to marinate meats and vegetables prior to roasting or grilling.

For *recados* to realize their full potential, they need salsas to provide counterpoint. Mix and match your favorite meat, fish, or poultry with a complementary *recado* and salsa. Take a chicken breast, perhaps, and marinate it in one of the *recados*. Grill it and top with one of the salsas, and you have an easy and terrific meal.

# Do:

Use achiote with fruitier-tasting salsas such as Charred Habanero Salsa (page 39), Tropical Fruit Salsa (page 45), and Charred Tomato Mint Salsa (page 37).

Use Chipotle Rub (page 31) and Garlic Rub (page 29) with the hotter, more savory salsas such as Avocado Árbol Salsa (page 44), Grilled Jalapeño Salsa (page 37), Green Chile Salsa (page 39), and Norteño-Style Árbol Chile Salsa (page 38).

Use wet marinades on foods that dry out easily, such as pork, chicken, lean beef, and fish.

Use dry rubs on foods with naturally high fat or moisture content, including steaks, tuna, and dark-meat poultry.

Combine *recados* and salsas with similar ingredients such as Pumpkin Seed Recado (page 32) and Pumpkin Seed Salsa (page 42), Chipotle Rub (page 31), and any of the dried-chile salsas.

# Don't:

Overmarinate food in the *recados*. The food could become too salty or even dry out, as salt draws moisture out of food.

Worry! The more experience you gain trying different combinations—and when something pleases you, remember it!—the more the underlying harmonies of Mexican cooking will become apparent.

*Recados* tend to stick like mad to the grill. There are ways to deal with this: Liberally oil your grill ahead of time and/or invest in grill liners or racks that will make cleanup a bit easier. But don't worry, *recados* are meant to char and stick a bit.

**Here are some dos and don'ts for**

**combining *recados*, salsas,**

**and food for the grill:**

## Traditional Achiote Recado

2 tablespoons annatto seeds

½ cup water

1 teaspoon freshly ground allspice

2 teaspoons freshly ground black pepper

½ cup ancho chile powder

4 teaspoons kosher salt

1 tablespoon toasted and ground dried Mexican oregano

3 cloves garlic, pan-roasted until brown and soft, then peeled

½ medium-sized white onion, thickly sliced, pan-roasted until brown and soft

¼ cup pineapple vinegar or apple cider vinegar

1½ cups freshly squeezed orange juice

¼ cup freshly squeezed lemon juice

*This mild, citrusy red spice paste can transform the blandest of foods. It comes from the Yucatán, where it typically flavors Pibil-style suckling pig. The pig is rubbed with the* recado, *wrapped in banana leaves, and then cooked in a stone-lined pit until the meat is so tender it falls off the bones. Grilling is a less traditional, but no less delicious, method. Use for meat, fish, and poultry. Purchased achiote paste saves a good deal of time and makes a less complex but acceptable* recado.

**Makes about 2½ cups.**

Put the annatto seeds and water in a small saucepan and place over high heat. Bring to a boil, cover, and lower heat to a simmer. Cook 30 minutes. Remove from heat and let steep 2 hours, or until softened. Drain and put in a blender or food processor along with all the remaining ingredients. Blend until smooth. Keeps, tightly covered, up to 5 days in the refrigerator.

## Quick Achiote Recado

6 tablespoons achiote paste

¾ cup freshly squeezed orange juice

2 tablespoons freshly squeezed lemon juice

**Makes about 1¼ cups.**

Put all the ingredients in a food processor and process until mixture is free of lumps. Keeps, tightly covered, up to 5 days in the refrigerator.

# Tamarind Recado

*Smoky, sweet, sour, and earthy, this recado is great on shrimp and pork and can be used for beef and venison as well. Although you can use prepared tamarind pulp, you will have a tastier result by following my method for preparing fresh tamarind pulp on page 16.*

**Makes about 3 cups.**

Heat the corn oil in a small skillet over medium-high heat until hot but not smoking. Fry the chiles, 1 or 2 at a time, until puffed and brown, about 10 seconds. Do not let them burn or they will be bitter. Shake off excess oil and put the chiles in a small bowl. Add the boiling water and let soak until soft, about 20 minutes. Toss occasionally to make sure all the chiles soften evenly.

Put the softened chiles, ½ cup of the chile soaking water, and all the remaining ingredients in a blender or food processor and blend until smooth. Keeps, tightly covered, up to 5 days in the refrigerator.

2 tablespoons corn oil

6 chipotle chiles, seeded and deveined

1 cup boiling water

1½ cups tamarind pulp

1 medium-sized white onion, thickly sliced, pan-roasted until brown and soft

10 cloves garlic, pan-roasted until brown and soft, then peeled

4 Roma (plum) tomatoes, pan-roasted until blistered, deeply browned, and soft

1 tablespoon kosher salt

# Garlic Rub

*Keep a jar of this by the stove to use as a sophisticated garlic salt. At Café Marimba, we use it as a cure on pork, but it will give a very Mexican accent to almost any food, and is perfect for a thick steak. Season foods an hour or two in advance of grilling to let the* recado's *flavor penetrate.*

**Makes about 1 cup.**

Grind together in a spice mill the allspice, oregano, cumin, and cloves until you have a fine powder. Put the spices in a food processor with the garlic, salt, and pepper and process until you have a shaggy, saltlike spice rub.

If the mixture seems wet, spread it in a thin, even layer on a dry baking sheet. Let dry in a cool (150°F) oven until no longer moist, about 1 hour. You will be able to break up any lumps with your fingers. Store at room temperature in a covered container indefinitely. Regrind the rub before use, if necessary.

10 whole allspice

2 tablespoons dried Mexican oregano, toasted

2 tablespoons cumin seeds, toasted

4 whole cloves

10 cloves garlic, pan-roasted until brown and soft, then peeled

½ cup kosher salt

1 tablespoon freshly ground black pepper

# Chipotle Rub

*Some recados are wet pastes. Some are more like dry rubs, including this one. It gives a burst of flavor to almost any vegetable or meat, but is particularly wonderful on beef and corn. In the past I made it with chipotles only. Tim Anderson, Café Marimba's corporate chef, decided to add anchos while grilling corn for a street fair. Anchos have a sweeter flavor and give the recado a pretty, paprikalike color and more dimension than chipotles alone. I always make it Tim's way now.*

**Makes about 3¼ cups.**

¼ cup corn oil

5 chipotle chiles, seeded and deveined

5 ancho chiles, seeded and deveined

25 cloves garlic

1½ cups kosher salt

¼ cup dried Mexican oregano, toasted

Heat the corn oil in a medium-sized sauté pan over medium-high heat until hot but not smoking. Fry the chiles, 1 or 2 at a time, until they are puffed and brown, about 10 seconds. Do not let them burn or the rub will be bitter. Drain the chiles on paper towels and set aside until they are cool and crisp. (Discard the oil or save in a jar to add to soups, stews, and sauces.)

Grind the chiles in batches in a spice mill until they are a fine powder. Place the ground chiles and all the remaining ingredients in a food processor and process until you have a shaggy, saltlike spice rub. If the mixture seems wet, spread it in a thin, even layer on a dry baking sheet. Let dry in a cool (150°F) oven until no longer moist, about 1 hour. You will be able to break up any lumps with your fingers. Store at room temperature in a covered container indefinitely. Regrind the rub before use, if necessary.

# Mint Recado

*This brightly flavored recado marries well with goat and lamb and is also very nice on fish such as fresh sardines or sea bass. Cut slashes in the meat or fish and press the recado into the flesh. Let sit an hour or so, covered and refrigerated, before grilling.*

**Makes about ¾ cup.**

1 medium-sized white onion

40 fresh mint leaves

½ cup fresh cilantro leaves

2 teaspoons kosher salt

2 teaspoons freshly ground black pepper

8 whole allspice, freshly ground

Finely chop the onion, mint, and cilantro together by hand or pulse together in a food processor. The ingredients should all be chopped the same size. Transfer to a bowl and mix in the salt, pepper, and allspice. Use immediately.

# Pumpkin Seed Recado

1/3 cup olive oil

1/2 cup pumpkin seeds

1 clove garlic, minced

2 tablespoons minced white onion

1/4 cup minced fresh cilantro

2 fresh epazote leaves, minced (optional)

1 teaspoon cumin seeds, toasted and then ground

1 jalapeño chile with seeds, minced

1/2 teaspoon kosher salt

*This pumpkin seed paste is so delicious you will have a hard time not eating it plain. Serve it as a dip, or on grilled fish, vegetables, or poultry. It sets off the richness of duck especially well. Press a thick layer of the paste onto foods and let sit, covered and refrigerated, an hour or more to allow the subtle flavors to be absorbed.*

**Makes about 3/4 cup.**

Heat the olive oil in a small skillet over medium-high heat until hot but not smoking. Add the pumpkin seeds and cook, swirling the pan and stirring often, until the seeds are evenly toasted. They will puff and pop. Using a slotted spoon, transfer to paper towels to drain.

Grind pumpkin seeds in a food processor until finely chopped. Add all the remaining ingredients and continue to process until well blended. Keeps, tightly covered, up to 3 days in the refrigerator.

# Adobo Recado

*Adobo could be called Mexican barbecue sauce. Just about every cook has his or her personal version. The balance of ingredients shifts by region as well. Adobo was originally used to preserve meat: The paste was smeared on strips of meat, which were then hung up to dry. For a hotter version, leave the seeds and veins of the chiles in, although you will then lose the subtle contrast of flavors that is the soul of adobo. The final frying of the sauce pulls the flavors together and adds a smokiness.*

**Makes about 2½ cups.**

Heat the oil in a medium-sized sauté pan over medium-high heat until hot but not smoking. Fry the chiles, 1 or 2 at a time, until puffed and brown, about 10 seconds. Do not let them burn or the adobo will taste bitter. Shake off excess oil from the chiles and place in a medium bowl. Reserve the cooking oil. Add the boiling water to the chiles and let soak until soft, about 20 minutes. Toss occasionally to make sure all the chiles soften evenly.

Put the softened chiles, their soaking water, and all the remaining ingredients in a blender and blend until smooth. (You can use a food processor, but you will not get as smooth a texture.)

Heat 2 tablespoons of reserved chile oil in a large nonstick skillet over medium-high heat until hot but not smoking. Pour the blended mixture into the skillet and cook, stirring frequently, until it begins to reduce, sizzle, and becomes darkly colored, about 10 minutes. If it boils too vigorously, lower the heat. Keeps, tightly covered, several weeks in the refrigerator.

**1 cup corn oil**

**6 guajillo chiles, seeded and deveined**

**4 ancho chiles, seeded and deveined**

**1 chipotle chile, seeded and deveined**

**1 cup boiling water**

**8 whole allspice, freshly ground**

**4 whole cloves, freshly ground**

**1 teaspoon cumin seeds, freshly ground**

**1 tablespoon dried Mexican oregano, freshly ground**

**5 cloves garlic**

**2 tablespoons sugar**

**2 Roma (plum) tomatoes, pan-roasted until blistered, deeply browned, and soft**

**½ cup apple cider vinegar**

**½ teaspoon freshly ground pepper**

**1 teaspoon kosher salt**

# salsas

# I like to think

that composition in food is like composition in music. Harmony, counterpoint, tempo, and intensity are vital components to a pleasing composition. Salsa is the vibrant counterpoint of Mexican food. Colorful, richly layered, and exciting, it soars against the driving backbeat of *recado*-scented grilled foods.

Salsas are both casual and deeply important, just like salsa music. They come together with otherwise uninteresting foods and make them lively—literally, brilliant. If the only salsa you have ever tasted is the stuff that comes in cans and jars (whether it is made in El Paso or New York City), you haven't had salsa. Canned salsa is like Lawrence Welk Latin music: It may work for some in a pinch, but I'd rather just do without.

Try making these salsas. They are easy, and once you master the pre-Hispanic technique of pan-roasting, you can be a virtuoso at improvising new salsas to suit your mood and the occasion. Just remember, respect fundamental harmonies. No sun-dried tomato, ginger, and chipotle salsa, please!

# Charred Tomato Mint Salsa

*To some people, cilantro tastes soapy. Many Yucatecans must share this feeling, as they often use mint to balance the strong flavor of cilantro. This bright, minty salsa will appeal to cilantro lovers and detractors alike. To appreciate its flavors fully, use ripe summer tomatoes.*

**Makes about 1 cup.**

Chop together with a knife or food processor the tomatoes, onion, and garlic until you have a coarsely textured salsa. Add the chiles, cilantro, mint, cumin, water, and salt. Process briefly to mix; the salsa should be chunky. Keeps, tightly covered, up to 2 days in the refrigerator.

3 Roma (plum) tomatoes, pan-roasted until blistered, deeply browned, and soft

1 thick slice medium-sized white onion, pan-roasted until brown and soft

1 medium-sized clove garlic, pan-roasted until brown and soft, then peeled

2 serrano chiles with seeds, roughly chopped

12 fresh cilantro leaves, coarsely chopped

3 large fresh mint leaves, finely chopped

¼ teaspoon toasted and ground cumin

¼ cup water

⅛ teaspoon kosher salt

# Grilled Jalapeño Salsa

*This salsa makes lavish use of the most popular hot chile, the jalapeño, whose meaty, rich flavor complements a wide variety of foods. But beware: In terms of heat, jalapeños and poblanos are the most inconsistent chiles on the market. Taste them before you start a recipe so you know what you are getting into. The texture of this salsa is very important. It should be coarse and a little stringy. You can make it in a food processor, pulsing quickly (it helps if you have a dull blade), but it is best made by hand in a* molcajete.

**Makes about 1¼ cups.**

Put all the ingredients in a *molcajete* or food processor and blend very briefly until you have a very chunky sauce. Use the same day it is made.

16 jalapeño chiles, pan-roasted until dark brown, seeded, deveined (skin left on), then coarsely chopped

2 Roma (plum) tomatoes, pan-roasted until blistered, deeply browned, and soft

1 thick slice medium-sized white onion, pan-roasted until dark brown and soft, then coarsely chopped

½ cup water

¼ teaspoon kosher salt

¼ teaspoon toasted and ground dried Mexican oregano

## Norteño-Style Árbol Chile Salsa

¼ cup corn oil

6 árbol chiles, with seeds

8 tomatillos, husked

1 small clove garlic, minced

1 tablespoon coarsely chopped fresh cilantro

½ cup water

⅓ cup finely diced white onion

⅛ teaspoon kosher salt

⅛ teaspoon toasted and ground dried Mexican oregano

⅛ teaspoon toasted and ground cumin

*In northern Mexico and south Texas, this brick-red salsa is slathered over all kinds of meats and cheeses. In fact, this style of salsa became so popular that variations (like Tabasco sauce) are bottled for sale worldwide. Try this version for its complex and cleansing heat.*

**Makes about 1¼ cups.**

Heat the corn oil in a medium-sized skillet over medium-high heat until hot but not smoking. Fry the chiles, 1 or 2 at a time, until puffed and brown, about 10 seconds. Do not burn or they will taste bitter. Shake off excess oil from chiles and place in a food processor.

Put the tomatillos in a small saucepan, cover with water, and place over high heat. Bring to a boil, lower heat to a simmer, and cook until tender, about 10 minutes. The tomatillos will have changed color and be soft but still whole.

Add the tomatillos to the food processor along with the garlic. Process until finely chopped. Add the cilantro and water and continue to process until smooth. Add the onion, salt, oregano, and cumin and pulse to mix. Keeps, tightly covered, about 3 days in the refrigerator.

## Tomato Árbol Salsa

¼ cup corn oil

12 árbol chiles, with seeds

2 Roma (plum) tomatoes, pan-roasted until blistered, deeply browned, and soft

6 medium-sized cloves garlic, pan-roasted until brown and soft, then peeled

¾ cup water

¼ teaspoon dried Mexican oregano, toasted

¼ teaspoon kosher salt

¼ teaspoon toasted and ground cumin

*This is typical of what you would find on tables in northern Mexico, where salsas tend to be a little brutal—hot and very direct with uncomplicated flavors. I love this kind of salsa on quesadillas and broiled meats. A great all-purpose condiment, a spoonful or two will enliven almost any dish. Be careful, though. People in the north like their food hot.*

**Makes about 1½ cups.**

Heat the corn oil in a medium-sized skillet until hot but not smoking. Fry the chiles, 1 or 2 at a time, until puffed and brown, about 10 seconds. Do not burn or they will taste bitter. Shake off excess oil from chiles and place in a blender. Add 2 tablespoons chile cooking oil, tomatoes, garlic, and water. Blend until smooth. Add the oregano, salt, and cumin and blend again. Keeps, tightly covered, about 3 days in the refrigerator.

# Charred Habanero Salsa

*Salsas in the Yucatán are usually quite simple, while recados tend to make the dishes they season complex. Perhaps that is why simplicity is seen as a virtue when it comes to salsas. But I think there is another reason: the habanero chile, reputedly the hottest pepper in the world. In addition to the heat, habaneros have a citrusy aroma and flavor that are best savored on their own. This salsa is the classical accompaniment to meats and seafood cooked in achiote. Try it on Grilled Squid Yucatán Style (page 64). There are variations with onion, orange juice, and mint, but this simple version is my favorite.*

**Makes about 1 cup.**

Put all the ingredients in a blender and blend until smooth. Use within several hours.

3 Roma (plum) tomatoes, pan-roasted until blistered, deeply browned, and soft

3 habanero chiles, pan-roasted until dark brown, then seed cores removed

¼ cup water

⅛ teaspoon kosher salt

# Green Chile Salsa

*Green chiles—poblanos, Anaheims, and New Mexico long greens—always make me think of Santa Fe. There, they make salsa with the local chiles and bottle it for sale around the world. This fresh version has more complex seasonings than the Santa Fe product, and is one of the truly great salsas for dipping and slathering all over everything.*

**Makes about 1¼ cups.**

Place the garlic, onion, tomato, tomatillo, and chiles in a food processor and pulse briefly until finely chopped. Add the water, cilantro, salt, and cumin and process again until blended. Keeps, tightly covered, about 3 days in the refrigerator.

1 clove garlic, pan-roasted until brown and soft, then peeled

1 thick slice medium-sized white onion, pan-roasted until brown and soft, then roughly chopped

1 Roma (plum) tomato, pan-roasted until blistered, deeply browned, and soft

1 tomatillo, pan-roasted until blistered, browned, and soft

3 poblano chiles, pan-roasted until dark brown, then seed cores removed

½ cup water

1 tablespoon roughly chopped fresh cilantro

⅛ teaspoon kosher salt

¼ teaspoon toasted and ground cumin

# Green Chile Mushroom Salsa

*I have seen fresh morels in Mexico City markets around Christmas, and other wild mushrooms are abundant elsewhere in Mexico after the rains. This extravagant salsa is pure heaven on a thick steak seasoned with Chipotle Rub (page 31) and grilled over mesquite. For the best results, have all the ingredients at approximately the same temperature when you make the salsa—the mushrooms still warm from sautéing, and the chiles, tomatoes, and garlic still warm from pan-roasting. If morels are unavailable, other wild mushrooms can be substituted.*

**Makes about 1½ cups.**

½ ounce dried morels or ¼ pound fresh morels

1 tablespoon olive oil

2 poblano chiles, pan-roasted until dark brown, then seed cores removed

2 Roma (plum) tomatoes, pan-roasted until blistered, deeply browned, and soft

3 medium-sized cloves garlic, pan-roasted until brown and soft, then peeled

6 fresh epazote leaves, chopped

½ cup water

⅛ teaspoon kosher salt

Place dried morels in a small bowl, cover with water, and let soak until soft, about 15 minutes. Drain, reserving soaking liquid, and cut in half. If using fresh morels, wipe clean and cut in half.

Heat the olive oil in a small skillet over medium-high heat until hot but not smoking. Add the fresh or dried morels and sauté until lightly browned, about 1 minute. (If using dried mushrooms, now strain the mushroom-soaking liquid over the mushrooms, bring to a boil, and cook until the pan is again dry.) Continue to sauté until mushrooms are browned, about 3 minutes.

Put the morels in a food processor with the poblanos, tomatoes, garlic, and epazote. Pulse until coarsely chopped; do not purée. Scrape into a bowl and stir in the water and salt. Taste for seasoning. Keeps, tightly covered, about 3 days in the refrigerator.

# Pico de Gallo

*Pico de gallo ("beak of the rooster" in Spanish) is perhaps the most common salsa in Mexico, and also one of the simplest and most accessible. It is made with only four raw ingredients: chiles, tomato, onion, and cilantro. Sometimes you will see it without tomato, or without cilantro, and sometimes with the addition of avocado.*

**Makes about 2 cups.**

3 jalapeño chiles with seeds, roughly chopped

1 medium-sized tomato, chopped

1 cup roughly chopped white onion

¼ cup roughly chopped fresh cilantro

¼ teaspoon kosher salt

2 tablespoons water

Mix all the ingredients together in a small, nonreactive bowl. Let sit a few minutes to develop the flavors before using. Keeps, tightly covered, up to 2 days in the refrigerator.

## Ripe Chile Salsa

3 red, ripe New Mexico chiles or 2 or 3 red, ripe poblano chiles, roasted and peeled, then seed cores removed

3 medium-sized cloves garlic, pan-roasted until brown and soft, then peeled

¾ cup hot water

1 teaspoon apple cider vinegar

1 tablespoon oil from frying chiles (if you have it) or corn oil

⅛ teaspoon kosher salt

*In the late summer, a variety of hot chiles ripen on the vine, and they are typically hung and dried to become the familiar wrinkled pods. But in this month-long season, you can also often find them fresh, so grab a bunch and make this salsa. Or just char and peel them as you would red bell peppers and marinate them in oil as a garnish for broiled meats or even pizza. When ripe chiles are not available, use 1 large red bell pepper and 2 tablespoons ancho chile powder in their place. It is very good as well and a perfect accompaniment for pork.*

**Makes about 1½ cups.**

Put all the ingredients in a food processor and process until smooth. Let sit 30 minutes to develop the flavors. Keeps, tightly covered, up to 4 days in the refrigerator.

## Pumpkin Seed Salsa

4 teaspoons olive oil or corn oil

½ cup pumpkin seeds

1 Roma (plum) tomato, pan-roasted until blistered, deeply browned, and soft

1 thick slice medium-sized white onion, pan-roasted until brown and soft

1 tomatillo, pan-roasted until blistered, browned, and soft

2 jalapeño chiles, pan-roasted until dark brown, then seed cores removed

1 large clove garlic, pan-roasted until brown and soft, then peeled

½ cup water

⅛ teaspoon kosher salt

1 tablespoon coarsely chopped fresh cilantro

⅛ teaspoon toasted and ground dried Mexican oregano

*I don't know why—in this land of pumpkin pie—we do not eat more of these great little seeds. Your local health food stores and Mexican markets will have the bright green hulled seeds for sale. Buy a lot and keep them in the freezer until you want to make this salsa, or toast them together with chiles pequíns (tiny, round dried red chiles) and whole garlic cloves as a snack. Try this delicate salsa over broiled goat cheese or stirred into white rice just before serving. Then again, you might want to ladle it on some simple grilled chicken. Just try it.*

**Makes about 1½ cups.**

Heat the oil in a small skillet over medium-high heat until hot but not smoking. Add the pumpkin seeds and cook, swirling the pan and stirring often, until evenly toasted, about 2 minutes. They will puff and pop. Scrape the seeds and their oil into a food processor and add the tomato, onion, and tomatillo. Process until smooth. Add the jalapeños and garlic, and continue to process. With the motor running, add the water. Stop to scrape down the sides. Add the salt, cilantro, and oregano, and pulse to blend. Keeps, tightly covered, up to 3 days in the refrigerator.

# Authentic Guacamole

*Everybody knows how to make guacamole, right? Wrong. Please, no lime or lemon, no sour cream. This recipe makes what is probably the most commonly made guacamole in Mexico. It is very rich and buttery, and is so simple to make, it can be done at the last minute. We make guacamole to order at Café Marimba, adding a little cilantro and roasted tomato, and we serve it right in the* molcajete *in which it is made.*

**Makes about 1 cup.**

Quickly mash the avocados and chiles together and season with salt. Guacamole should be chunky. Taste for seasoning and serve immediately.

2 ripe avocados, halved, pitted, and spooned into a bowl

3 serrano chiles or 1 jalapeño chile, with seeds, finely minced

Scant ⅛ teaspoon kosher salt

# Taqueria Guacamole

*This is the version of guacamole you often see in little taquerias in Mexico. The spicy, thin mixture has a great smooth flavor. But the reason you see it used so often is that it is much less expensive than the famous chunky guacamole, an advantage in tiny restaurants where tacos commonly cost less than the equivalent of thirty cents. It is so good, however, that I use it even when the difference in cost is no object.*

**Makes about 2 cups.**

Put all the ingredients except the onion in a food processor and blend until very smooth. Pour into a bowl and stir in the onion. Use immediately.

1 jalapeño chile, with seeds

3 tablespoons coarsely chopped fresh cilantro

1 ripe avocado, peeled and pitted

¼ teaspoon kosher salt

1 cup water

3 tablespoons diced white onion

## Avocado Árbol Salsa

1 tablespoon corn oil

4 árbol chiles, with seeds

1 small handful fresh cilantro

1 ripe avocado

1 cup cold water

¼ teaspoon kosher salt

½ teaspoon toasted and ground avocado leaf (optional)

*Some flavor combinations seem natural for a salsa, such as jalapeño, cilantro, and tomato. Others, like rich avocado and toasty, insistently picante árbol chile, are a revelation. Try this unusual Oaxacan salsa on almost any grilled meat, as well as on mild white fish. And if you can find some avocado leaf (see Sources), do add it. It brings out that haunting anise aroma that is just below the surface of avocado. Superb.*

**Makes about 1 ¾ cups.**

Heat the corn oil in a small skillet over medium-high heat until hot but not smoking. Fry the chiles, 1 or 2 at a time, until puffed and brown, about 10 seconds. Shake off excess oil and put the chiles in a food processor. Add the cilantro, avocado, water, salt, and, if using, avocado leaf. Process until smooth. Make just before serving.

## Fragrant Salsa

1 tablespoon corn oil

1 chipotle chile, seeded and deveined

1 pasilla chile, seeded and deveined

1 ancho chile, seeded and deveined

1 cup boiling water

1 small fresh or dried *hierba santa* leaf

1 slice small white onion (1 inch thick), pan-roasted until brown and soft

1 medium-sized clove garlic, pan-roasted until brown and soft, then peeled

Small pinch of toasted and ground cumin

¼ teaspoon kosher salt

1¼ cups warm water

*The aroma of toasted chiles and* hierba santa *is a haunting reminder of Oaxacan culture—a great culture now only dimly visible in the native foods and crafts. Use this as an all-purpose table salsa. It is particularly good on white meats, fish, and cheese. You can also use it as a marinade or as cooking liquid for braising rabbit or other meats. Many salsas are very good when used in these ways.*

**Makes about 1½ cups.**

Heat the corn oil in a small skillet over medium-high heat until hot but not smoking. Fry the chiles, 1 or 2 at a time, until puffed and brown, about 10 seconds. Do not burn or they will taste bitter. Shake off excess oil and place the chiles in a small bowl. Add the boiling water and let soak until soft, about 20 minutes. Toss occasionally to make sure all the chiles soften evenly.

Drain the softened chiles and put in a blender or food processor with the *hierba santa*, onion, garlic, cumin, salt, and water. Process until smooth. Keeps, tightly covered, about 3 days in the refrigerator.

# Tropical Fruit Salsa

*The most commonly seen salsa in the Yucatán is a little bowl of sliced habanero chiles covered with the juice of sour orange. This is a more complex version of that salsa, and it is a real delight. Try it when you have a taste for something tropical. Smear a whole fresh sierra fish or tuna fillet with an achiote recado and grill it over a wood fire on the beach. Stuff corn tortillas with the fish and some of this sunny salsa, perch yourself on a piece of driftwood, and enjoy some fabulous tacos.*

**Makes about 3½ cups.**

The skin of bell peppers can be tough, so it is often a good idea to peel them. Pull off the stem and remove the seed core. Cut lengthwise between the lobes, cut out the veins, and shake out any seeds. Peel each section of outer skin with a sharp, swivel-bladed vegetable peeler. Cut into ⅛-inch dice. Mix all the ingredients together in a small nonreactive bowl and let sit 30 minutes before serving. Use the salsa the same day it is made.

**1 small red bell pepper**

**1 cup chopped ripe papaya**

**1 cup chopped ripe mango**

**2 habanero chiles with seeds, diced**

**1 tablespoon roughly chopped fresh cilantro**

**1 cup freshly squeezed orange juice**

**1 tablespoon freshly squeezed lime juice**

**2 fresh mint leaves, coarsely chopped**

**1 scallion, white and green parts, finely sliced**

# Grilled Pineapple Salsa

*I like the idea of salsas that don't require a lot of fussing around in the kitchen while you are grilling outdoors, and this one fits that bill. Pineapple can be cloying alongside savory foods, but grilling caramelizes the sugary fruit into a nutty sweetness and it becomes a great match for fish and seafood. Add the smoky heat of the chipotle chile and you have one of my favorite salsas.*

**Makes about 1½ cups.**

Light the grill. Brush the onion and pineapple slices with 1 tablespoon of the oil. Place slices on grill over a medium-hot fire and grill until caramelized and browned all over, about 10 minutes.

Heat the remaining tablespoon oil in a small skillet over medium-high heat until hot but not smoking. Add the chile and fry until puffed and brown, about 10 seconds. Shake off excess oil and place in a food processor. Cut the onion and pineapple into chunks, discarding pineapple cores, and add to food processor with mint, cilantro, water, and lime juice. Process until uniformly chopped. Use the same day it is made.

**2 slices white onion (1 inch thick)**

**2 slices pineapple (1 inch thick), peeled**

**2 tablespoons corn oil**

**1 chipotle chile, with seeds**

**2 fresh mint leaves, chopped**

**1 teaspoon coarsely chopped fresh cilantro**

**½ cup water**

**Juice of ½ lime**

8 tomatillos, husked and chopped

2 jalapeño chiles with seeds, chopped

1 small handful fresh cilantro leaves

¼ cup water

½ small white onion, chopped

¼ teaspoon kosher salt

## Tomatillo Salsa

*I have often said that salsas provide counterpoint—that is, they contrast with the foods they accompany, rather than taste like them. No salsa is a more obvious or ubiquitous example than this tomatillo salsa. The sour, astringent, green-plum flavor of the tomatillo nicely sets off bland or rich foods. To see what I mean, try a little on a piece of mild cheese or chicken breast. This is Mexican cooking in pure voice.*

**Makes about 2 cups.**

Put the tomatillos, chiles, cilantro, and water in a blender and blend until very smooth. Pour into a medium-sized nonreactive bowl, and stir in the onion and salt. Use the same day it is made.

4 pasilla chiles

1 tomatillo, pan-roasted until blistered, browned, and soft

1 large Roma (plum) tomato, pan-roasted until blistered, deeply browned, and soft

3 cloves garlic, pan-roasted until brown and soft, then peeled

¼ teaspoon dried Mexican oregano, toasted

¼ teaspoon salt

1 cup water

## Soledad's Salsa

*This salsa is often on the table of my friend Soledad's restaurant, El Topil, in Oaxaca. It complements all kinds of foods, from cheese to fish and chicken.*

**Makes about 1½ cups.**

Heat a small, heavy skillet over medium heat. Add the chiles and toast, pressing them into the pan with a spatula, until brown and fragrant, about 10 seconds. Break off the stems and discard with the seeds. Put the chiles and all the remaining ingredients in a blender. Process at high speed until you have a coarsely textured liquid.

# Veracruz Salsa

*This smoky, spicy salsa is widely used around Veracruz as an all-purpose accompaniment to fish and seafood dishes. Its rich flavor is the perfect counterpoint to sweet shellfish and fruity lime. Try stirring a little into a bowl of soup or even a Bloody Mary cocktail.*

**Makes about 2 cups.**

Heat the oil in a skillet over medium-high heat until hot but not smoking. Add the chiles, a few at a time, and cook until puffed and just beginning to brown, about 10 seconds. Shake off excess oil. Put the chiles in a blender with all the remaining ingredients and blend until very smooth. Keeps, tightly covered, up to 2 days in the refrigerator.

1 tablespoon corn oil

12 morita chiles or 8 chipotle chiles, with seeds

2 cloves garlic, pan-roasted until brown and soft, then peeled

1 tomato, pan-roasted until blistered, deeply browned, and soft

1½ cups hot water

¼ teaspoon kosher salt

# Salsa Butters

*Salsa is so versatile, I am always discovering new ways to use it. Try making a compound butter with your favorite salsa. Let it melt slowly over grilled or roasted fish, chicken, beef, or lamb. They are sinfully delicious. Also, try guacamole butter with a pile of grilled soft shell crabs. Yum!*

**Makes about ¾ cup.**

Put all the ingredients in a food processor and blend until butter and salsa are evenly blended. Scrape into a bowl and chill. Keeps, tightly covered and refrigerated, for up to 3 days.

8 tablespoons (1 stick) unsalted butter, softened

½ cup salsa such as Grilled Jalapeño Salsa (page 37), Green Chile Mushroom Salsa (page 41), Authentic Guacamole (page 43), or Norteño-Style Árbol Chile Salsa (page 38)

⅛ teaspoon kosher salt

seafood

# Many people seem

unaware of the quality and sophistication of Mexican seafood cookery. I was fortunate a few years ago to have the opportunity to visit both the Italian Riviera and Veracruz within the same month. No one would deny that the sea bass, roasted with potatoes, wine, olive oil, and olives, was to die for in Portofino. What surprises a lot of people, though, is that the quality of the fish and its preparation were as good, if not better, in Veracruz.

Top-quality fish has a purity that demands respect. By careful use of *recados* and salsas, the pristine quality of the fish is heightened. A grilled whole lobster lightly dusted with a chipotle-based rub and smothered in garlic and lime is simplicity close to heaven. Wrapping salmon in corn husks along with corn and spices may be more complex but no less exquisite. Try these fish dishes and see if you don't agree about the quality of the Mexican approach to seafood.

## Shrimp with Tamarind Recado

*This perfect appetizer was inspired by dishes created by Alicia De'Angeli, a food writer and consultant in Mexico City, and Mark Miller of Coyote Café, in Santa Fe. I have combined their ideas to come up with this great little dish. Serve it to your friends at your next cookout. Buy some extra tamarind and make tamarindo, a refreshing cooler that mixes tamarind with water, ice, sugar, lime juice, and rum (if you like; I do). Accompany the shrimp with Oaxacan-Style Black Beans with Avocado Leaves (page 106). Recados, especially those made with tamarind, typically include vegetables and fruits that contain lots of natural sugars. This makes them susceptible to caramelization on the grill, which tastes great.*

**Serves 4.**

Light the grill. In a medium-sized nonreactive bowl, toss the shrimp with the *recado* and let marinate until the grill is ready. Generously oil the grill and cook shrimp over a very hot fire until crusty, opaque, and charred, about 4 minutes. Serve immediately with the salsa.

**1½ pounds large shrimp, peeled and deveined**

**1½ cups Tamarind Recado (page 29)**

**Oil for grill**

**Charred Habanero Salsa (page 39)**

## Mussels a la Plancha

*This is the simplest and purest way of eating mussels. This dish (minus the salsa) is familiar to diners at LuLu Restaurant in San Francisco, where we serve more than four hundred pounds of mussels a week. I know of no more perfect picnic dish. I can just see a beach, some cold beer, good friends, a beautiful day, and a big fire with a griddle or sheet of steel over it for cooking the mollusks. As the mussels open, their liquid hits the hot pan, boils, and smokes, imparting a smoky flavor to the shellfish.*

**Serves 4.**

Light the grill. When fire is very hot, put a griddle, a large cast-iron skillet, or even a steel plate over the fire to preheat. When your plancha is hot, put the mussels straight onto the metal. The mussels will begin to steam and fuss. While the mussels cook, heat the butter and salsa together in a small pan over medium-high heat until the mixture sizzles. Off the heat, add the lime juice, salt, and, if using, epazote. When the mussels have opened and cooked 1 to 3 minutes, scoop onto plates and drizzle with the butter mixture.

**2 pounds small mussels**

**½ pound (2 sticks) unsalted butter**

**¼ cup Veracruz Salsa (page 47)**

**Juice of 1 lime**

**Scant ¼ teaspoon salt**

**1 tablespoon chopped fresh epazote (optional)**

# Grilled Scallops in the Shell

2 tablespoons unsalted butter

16 scallops on the half shell

Pinch of Garlic Rub (page 29)

¼ cup Taqueria Guacamole (page 43)

¼ cup Grilled Pineapple Salsa (page 45)

*This is so simple: scallops in the shell—or out of the shell if your fishmonger cannot get you these gems intact—and two salsas. The dish is at home on any occasion, from a backyard cookout to a sit-down dinner. I once served it with great results at a formal dinner at the Caribou Club in Aspen with a 1985 Domaine de la Romanée-Conti Le Montrachet.*

**Serves 4.**

Light the grill. If you are using scallops on the shell, cut the butter into small bits and distribute among the scallop shells. Dust the scallops lightly with Garlic Rub. Put the scallops directly on grill over a hot fire and cook until liquid in shells evaporates and the insides of the shells begin to brown, about 3 minutes. If scallops are large, flip them in their shells once during cooking, or cover the grill. Do not overcook or scallops will be fibrous and rubbery.

If you are using scallops without their shells, oil the grill well. Melt half of the butter, brush the scallops with it, dust with Garlic Rub, and place the scallops directly on the grill. Cut up the remaining butter and put a small piece on each scallop as it comes off the grill.

Serve 4 scallops to each person, 2 topped with a dollop of guacamole and 2 topped with a dollop of pineapple salsa.

# Grilled Oysters with Black Pepper

6 tablespoons (¾ stick) unsalted butter

¼ cup minced fresh chives

24 oysters on the half shell

2 cups whole black peppercorns

½ cup whole allspice

Lime wedges

*This easy dish creates a lot of harsh smoke, so make sure you are in a well-ventilated area. In spite of the smoke, these oysters have a subtle flavor and are absolutely to die for. Make more than you think you will eat. If your neighbors come rushing to help douse the flames, offer them a few.*

**Serves 4.**

Light the grill. Melt the butter with the chives in a small saucepan. Spoon a little butter mixture over each oyster. When the fire is hot, pour the peppercorns and allspice directly into it. When the spices begin to smoke, put the oysters on the grill, partially cover grill, and let cook just until warm and plumped, about 2 minutes. Squeeze some lime over the oysters and serve with more lime wedges.

## Grilled Sardines with Mint Recado

*For those of you who have not had them, trust me: Fresh sardines are just about the best fish in the world to grill. Serve them whole with the bones in or—rather laboriously—fillet them. If you do not live on the West Coast and cannot get fresh sardines, use 1½ pounds small whole Spanish mackerel or fillets of tuna, blue fish, or other oily fish. This is the Mexican grill at its simple, pure best. Accompany the sardines with Oaxacan-Style Black Beans with Avocado Leaves (page 106).*

**Serves 4 to 6.**

Light the grill. In a medium-sized bowl, toss the sardines with the *recado* and the olive oil, and season generously with salt and pepper. Cover and marinate, refrigerated, 30 minutes.

Oil grill and cook fish over a hot fire until cooked through and slightly charred, about 10 minutes. Serve with salsa.

**12 whole sardines**

**½ cup Mint Recado (page 31)**

**2 tablespoons olive oil, plus more for oiling grill**

**Salt and freshly ground black pepper to taste**

**Tomatillo Salsa (page 46)**

## Mixiote of Shrimp and Nopales

*Mixiote is the papery outer membrane of the versatile maguey cactus or century plant. It is traditionally used to wrap meats prior to steaming and imparts a subtle, sappy cactus flavor. This contemporary version is inspired by a great dish at Las Mercedes Restaurant near the Camino Real Hotel in Mexico City. If you cannot find mixiote in your local Mexican grocery, use banana leaves. This dish is so suave, so sophisticated, but at the same time so primitive. This is Mexican cooking at its best. Serve with fresh tortillas and Rice with Mint (page 104).*

**Serves 4.**

Light the grill and let burn down to a medium fire. In the meantime, bring a pot of salted water to a boil, add the nopales and onion, and cook until just tender, about 3 minutes. Drain, rinse, put in a bowl, and let cool. Add the *recado* and shrimp and toss well. Spread mixiote sheets or banana leaves on a countertop and divide the shrimp mixture among them. Top each with an epazote leaf and then fold up into a tight square package. Wrap each package in aluminum foil. Put the bundles on the grill, cover grill, and cook until shrimp are cooked through, about 20 minutes. Remove packages from foil and serve out of mixiote or banana-leaf wrappers with avocado slices.

**3 cups cut-up nopales (½ by 1½ inches)**

**½ cup cut-up white onion (½ by 1½ inches)**

**1 cup Adobo Recado (page 33)**

**1 pound shrimp, peeled, deveined, and cut in half lengthwise**

**4 sheets mixiote or pieces of banana leaf, 10 by 15 inches**

**4 fresh epazote leaves**

**2 ripe avocados, peeled, pitted, and sliced about ⅜ inch thick**

## Charred Spiced Bonito Tacos

1 pound bonito, mackerel, or yellowfin tuna fillet, cut into 2-by-4-by-1-inch strips, or 1 small whole mackerel

2 tablespoons freshly squeezed lime juice, plus more, if necessary

¼ cup olive oil, plus more for oiling grill

2 tablespoons Chipotle Rub (page 31)

2 tablespoons diced radish

2 tablespoons very thinly sliced scallion, white and green parts

Charred Tomato Mint Salsa (page 37)

8 small tortillas, heated

*For some reason, small tunas like the bonito are not as popular fresh as the large yellowfin and bigeye tunas. Bonito has a delicate yet rich flavor. In this recipe, the fish is highly seasoned, grilled, and then broken up into pieces with the tines of a fork and used as the filling for tacos. The slight bitterness from the grilling combined with the smoky richness of the seasoned fish is a perfect excuse to experiment with several salsas as accompaniments. I particularly recommend Charred Tomato Mint Salsa (page 37). Another excellent accompaniment for this dish is Summer Tomato, Avocado, and Chile Salad (page 100). Don't forget to have plenty of soft, fresh tortillas on hand.*

**Serves 4.**

Light the grill. In a medium-sized, nonreactive bowl, toss the fish with lime juice, ¼ cup olive oil, and Chipotle Rub. Cover, refrigerate, and let marinate about 1 hour. Oil grill and cook fish over a hot fire until lightly charred and medium-rare (it should still be pink in the middle), about 3 minutes.

In a warm bowl (so fish does not cool too much), shred fish. Taste for seasoning and sprinkle with a little more Chipotle Rub and lime juice, if needed. Top with radish and scallion and serve warm with salsa and tortillas.

## Whole Fish Studded with Garlic

1 whole fish (2 to 3 pounds) such as red snapper, grouper, rock fish, cod, bluefish, or mackerel

¼ cup slivered garlic

¼ cup olive oil, plus more for oiling grill

Salt and freshly ground black pepper

2 avocados, peeled, pitted, and sliced

2 limes, cut into wedges

Fragrant Salsa (page 44)

Fresh cilantro sprigs for garnish

*Garlic and fish are natural flavor partners. This dish is for real lovers of garlic. The browned bits of garlic sticking out of the fish give it a fearsome look and an awesome aroma. Serve with plenty of fresh tortillas and Refried Black Beans with Plantains (page 107). This is a feast.*

**Serves 4.**

Light the grill. With the point of a paring knife, cut slashes about ½ inch long in the fish and ½ inch deep, spacing them about 1½ inches apart all over both sides of the fish. Stick a garlic sliver in each slit, leaving about half of each sliver poking out so that the garlic will brown as it grills. Rub fish with ¼ cup oil and season generously with salt and pepper. Grill over a hot fire until brown and crusty on both sides and cooked through, 10 to 15 minutes. Serve with the avocado, lime wedges, and salsa. Garnish with cilantro sprigs.

# Seared Spiced Tuna

*Pan de cabazon, "shark bread," is a favorite of the port of Campeche. This contemporary version uses tuna instead of shark, serving it along with the traditional smooth black beans, roasted tomatoes, and a refreshing, bittersweet salad of mango, blood oranges, and greens. The effect is the same as pan de cabazon, but lighter and cleaner in flavor. This is one of the most requested dishes I have served over the years.*

**Serves 4.**

First prepare the Oaxacan-Style Black Beans and Charred Habanero Salsa.

Light the grill and let burn down to a medium-hot fire. In the meantime, pull off the stem and remove the seed core from the bell pepper. Cut lengthwise between the lobes, cut out the veins, and shake out any seeds. Peel each section of outer skin with a sharp, swivel-bladed vegetable peeler. Chop the pepper; you should have ½ cup. In a medium-sized, nonreactive bowl, toss together with the mango, orange, frisée, endive, cilantro, and vinaigrette. Set aside.

Reheat the black beans. Heat the oil in a small skillet over medium heat until hot. Add the tortillas to the oil, 1 at a time, and fry on both sides until crisp, about 1 minute. Drain on paper towels, salt lightly, and keep warm.

Mix black pepper, coriander, cumin, and ¼ teaspoon salt together in a small bowl. Dip tuna in egg white, then roll it in the pepper mixture. Score tuna to mark ½-inch-thick slices. Oil grill and grill fish until cooked approximately ½ inch deep on each side, about 1 minute per side. You want to leave a 1-inch square of red, rare tuna in the center of each piece of fish.

To serve, place 2 tortillas on each plate. Spoon black beans onto tortillas. Slice tuna into ½-inch-thick slices and arrange tuna over beans. Top with a spoonful of salsa and some of the mango salad. Serve at once.

**Orange Vinaigrette:** *This is a great, all-purpose Mexican salad dressing.*

**Makes about ¼ cup.**

Mix all the ingredients together in a small, nonreactive bowl. Add salt and freshly ground black pepper to taste.

---

Oaxacan-Style Black Beans with Avocado Leaves (page 106)

Charred Habanero Salsa (page 39)

1 small red bell pepper

½ cup diced mango

1 small blood or regular orange, segmented

2 handfuls frisée (curly endive) or escarole

1 small head Belgian endive, cut into ¼-inch-thick rings

About 20 fresh cilantro leaves

¼ cup Orange Vinaigrette (recipe follows)

2 tablespoons corn oil, plus more for oiling grill

8 small tortillas

1 tablespoon cracked black pepper

1 tablespoon coriander seeds

1 tablespoon cumin seeds

¼ teaspoon salt, plus more to taste

2 egg whites, lightly beaten

1 pound fresh tuna fillet, cut into 2 pieces, about 2 by 2 by 6 inches each

---

1 tablespoon freshly squeezed orange juice

1 shallot, chopped

1 tablespoon pineapple vinegar or apple cider vinegar

2 tablespoons hazelnut oil or olive oil

1 fresh mint leaf, chopped

# Grilled Snapper with Charred Habanero Salsa

*If you grill the fish whole over banana leaves, this is* tikin xik, *a classic Yucatán dish. It tastes best made on a deserted beach with a banana leaf right off the tree and fish straight from the ocean. If you are not lucky enough to be on the beach, have a* Cuba libre *(a rum and Coke made the right way—lots of rum, ice, a little cola), plan your vacation, and cook this dish. You may omit the banana leaves and grill the fish fillets. Served with the salsa, this makes an elegant first course, or can be offered as a main dish accompanied with Oaxacan-Style Black Beans with Avocado Leaves (page 106).*

**Serves 4.**

Place the fish in a medium-sized, nonreactive container and pour achiote over it. Turn to coat well. Cover, refrigerate, and let marinate at least 2 hours.

Light the grill and let burn down to a medium fire. If using banana leaf, wash it well in hot water, and lay it, still damp, on the grill. Immediately lay fish, skin side down, on top of leaf. Cover grill and cook, without turning the fish over, until done, about 10 minutes. When fish is cooked, juices will be bubbling and you will be able to lift out the central bone easily. If you are not using banana leaf, oil grill, and immediately lay fish on grill, skin side down. Grill until fish is cooked a little more than halfway through, about 5 minutes. Turn and grill until fish is just cooked through, about 3 minutes more for a ¾-inch-thick fillet. Serve topped with salsa.

**1 medium-sized whole red snapper or grouper (1½ to 2 pounds), split in half through the stomach and butterflied, or 2 pounds firm white fish fillets such as red snapper, grouper, or sea bass**

**1 cup Traditional or Quick Achiote Recado (page 28)**

**1 piece banana leaf, 10 by 15 inches (optional)**

**Charred Habanero Salsa (page 39)**

# Grilled Whole Lobster

1 live lobster (about 2 pounds)

¼ cup olive oil

1 tablespoon Garlic Rub (page 29)

3 tablespoons unsalted butter

8 cloves garlic, thinly sliced

Juice of I lime

Fresh cilantro sprigs for garnish

Veracruz Salsa (page 47)

*In Mexico, the common lobster is the clawless spiny lobster. Avoid these and be grateful the Maine lobster is widely available in the United States. I have adopted a technique for grilling a lobster that is common in restaurant kitchens: First it is plunged into boiling water for exactly 3 minutes per pound, then cooled in ice water. This not only kills the lobster, but because the meat is partially cooked, it makes cutting and grilling it much easier. This beachfront combination of grilled lobster, lime, and garlic is unbeatable for a summer picnic. Serve with Refried Black Beans with Plantains (page 107) and, of course, plenty of fresh tortillas.*

**Serves 2.**

Light the grill. Bring a large pot of water to a boil, drop in the lobster, and cook exactly 3 minutes per pound. Remove immediately and plunge into ice water to stop cooking. (This step may be done a few hours ahead.)

Split the lobster in two down the middle of the back and head. Remove black vein and sand sac. Brush with 1 tablespoon olive oil and sprinkle with Garlic Rub. Place lobster halves on grill to one side of a hot fire, cover grill, and cook until warmed through and done, about 8 minutes. The juices in the shell should be boiling. Transfer lobster to a warmed serving dish.

Heat the butter and remaining 3 tablespoons olive oil in a small saucepan over medium-high heat. Add garlic and cook, stirring frequently, until butter foams and garlic turns nut brown, about 2 minutes. Off the heat, add lime juice and immediately pour over lobster. Garnish with cilantro and serve with salsa.

# Grilled Spiced Whole Crab

*If you are not accustomed to dealing with live crabs, this dish may seem overwhelming. Do not pass it up. Have your fishmonger clean the crabs for you. I know of no more delightful food experience than to roll up your sleeves and wade into a pile of great-tasting grilled crab. Be careful when you grill them. Do not let the shell blacken too much or the meat will dry out. Keep the crabs to one side of the fire, have another beer, and get a healthy appetite going.*

**Serves 4.**

If using live crabs, bring a large pot of salted water to a boil, drop in crabs, and cook exactly 3 minutes per pound. Remove immediately and plunge into ice water to stop cooking. (This step may be done a few hours ahead.)

Light the grill and let burn down to a medium fire. In the meatime, crack crabs at each joint so they will absorb marinade. Put them in a large, nonreactive bowl, pour achiote over, cover, refrigerate, and let marinate for 1 to 4 hours. Drain crabs, oil grill well, and cook crabs on covered grill until cooked through, about 8 minutes.

Heat the olive oil and butter in a small saucepan over medium-high heat. Add garlic and cook, stirring frequently, until butter foams and garlic turns nut brown, about 2 minutes. Off the heat, add lime juice. Serve this butter sauce as a dip with the crabs.

**2 live Dungeness crabs (2 to 3 pounds each)**

**2 cups Traditional or Quick Achiote Recado (page 28)**

**3 tablespoons olive oil, plus more for oiling grill**

**3 tablespoons unsalted butter**

**8 cloves garlic, thinly sliced**

**Juice of 1 lime**

## Grilled Clams in Banana Leaves

4 pieces banana leaf, about 12 by 15 inches each

4 pounds clams (Manila, littleneck, or steamer) or mussels

4 avocado leaves (optional)

¼ cup olive oil

Lime wedges

Veracruz Salsa (page 47)

*Mexican cooks have long wrapped foods in leaves and placed them over a hot fire to cook. When heated, banana leaves give off a wonderful anise aroma that marries well with small fresh clams or mussels. You may serve the clams still wrapped in the leaves. They need only a drizzle of olive oil, a squeeze of lime, and some salsa.*

**Serves 4.**

Light the grill and let burn down to a medium fire. In the meantime, wash the banana leaves well in hot water and lay them on a countertop. Arrange one-fourth of the clams in a pile in the center of each leaf. If using avocado leaves, add 1 to each package. Fold leaves over clams to make a sealed package. Wrap in aluminum foil, seam side up to allow easy checking for doneness later. Lay packages on grill, cover grill, and cook until clams open, 8 to 15 minutes, depending on heat and type of clam. The best way to check if clams have opened is to listen to the steam (you should hear bubbling and hissing) and to judge from looking at the size of the packages (they puff up). But don't fret, you can also unwrap a package and take a quick peek. Just make sure not to let too much steam escape. Remove the foil and serve the clams hot, still in their banana leaves. Provide olive oil, lime wedges, and salsa for dipping.

## Staked Yellowtail

1 yellowtail or tuna fillet (about 2 pounds)

2 tablespoons olive oil

¼ cup Chipotle Rub (page 31)

A length of untreated board, 6 by 15 by 2 inches, or a split log

Cotton or sisal twine, dampened with water

Tomatillo Salsa (page 46)

*Before there was metal in the New World for grill grates, fish and meat were often tied to stakes or branches and leaned over an open fire to cook. This dish is typical of that style. I first cooked it after some friends speared a fish while skin diving off the coast of Baja. There was no grill on hand, or much of anything to cook with other than some driftwood, string, matches, and a few pesos for beer and tortillas. While the experience was perfect, the dish is much improved by the addition of the Chipotle Rub and the salsa. Serve with fresh tortillas and Drunken Beans (page 104).*

**Serves 4 or 5.**

Light the grill. Oil the fish and sprinkle generously with Chipotle Rub. Tie fish to board with twine. Prop board to lean over fire. If you are using a small grill, simply position board so it straddles fire, 10 inches above the heat. Cook over a hot fire until done, about 30 minutes. Since there is no induction of heat from the hot grill, the fish cooks slowly. If you don't want to fuss with the board, you may simply grill the fish over a low fire for about 15 minutes. It won't, however, take on the same woody, smoky flavors that it does with the board. Serve with salsa.

## Grilled Sierra Stuffed in Cactus

*This dish combines the delicate flavor of sierra, a flounderlike fish, with the subtle, green-bean flavor of nopales and the heady anise aromas of banana and avocado leaves. The pre-Hispanic aesthetic comes through loud and clear. It is almost possible to see native Indians harvesting the leaves of three coastal plants to complement the best of tidal fishing. Please do not be daunted by the unusual sound of this dish.*

**Serves 2.**

Light the grill and let burn down to a slow fire. Bring a pot of salted water to a boil, add nopales and onion, and cook until just tender, about 3 minutes. Drain, rinse, and put in a small bowl. Add *recado*, toss well, and set aside.

Toast avocado leaves by holding over an open flame until fragrant, about 10 seconds. Liberally salt and pepper the fish. Arrange 3 avocado leaves in the center of the banana leaf. Top with half the nopales mixture, then the fish. Top with remaining nopales mixture, then avocado leaves. Fold up banana leaf to create a sealed package. Wrap tightly in aluminum foil, place over a medium fire, cover, and cook until fish is just opaque, about 20 minutes. Remove foil and serve on banana leaf accompanied by salsa.

**1 cup cut-up nopales (½ by 1½ inches)**

**½ cup cut-up white onion (½ by 1½ inches)**

**Salt and freshly ground black pepper**

**¾ cup Adobo Recado (page 33)**

**6 avocado leaves**

**1 piece banana leaf, 10 by 15 inches**

**1 small sierra or flounder (about 2 pounds), or 10 ounces fillet**

**Veracruz Salsa (page 47)**

## Swordfish à la Plancha

1 pound swordfish steaks, about ¾ inch thick

1 cup Chile Oil (recipe follows)

½ teaspoon Garlic Rub (page 29), or salt and freshly ground black pepper to taste

¼ cup dry white wine

¼ cup freshly squeezed lime juice

1 tablespoon finely chopped fresh flat-leaf parsley

Grilled Pineapple Salsa (page 45)

*In Zihuatanejo, a fresh-from-the-water swordfish is cleaned, layered in a fiery oil to soak up flavor, then cooked on the beach bum's sauté pan—a well-seasoned steel plancha or griddle. The rich, meaty fish is finished at the last minute in a cloud of steam as wine and lime juice are poured straight onto the griddle. The flesh comes out nicely glazed on the outside with just a touch of fiery chile flavor. Serve with tortillas and Refried Black Beans with Plantains (page 107).*

**Serves 2.**

Light the grill. Place the fish in a medium-sized, nonreactive bowl and pour all but 1 tablespoon of the oil over it. Turn to coat well. Cover, refrigerate, and let marinate at least 1 hour, turning frequently. Place griddle or large cast-iron skillet over medium-hot fire to preheat. When very hot, drain fish, season with garlic rub or salt and freshly ground pepper, and place on griddle. Be careful of flare-ups and blow out flames that may spontaneously ignite. Cook until crusty on one side, about 30 seconds. Turn and cook other side, about 1 minute more. Pour wine and lime juice over fish and cook until fish is glazed and liquid is almost evaporated, about 2 minutes. Turn fish frequently. Remove fish to a platter, drizzle with the reserved chile oil, sprinkle with parsley, and serve with salsa on the side.

2 guajillo chiles, seeded and deveined

2 ancho chiles, seeded and deveined

4 árbol chiles, including seeds

2 cups olive oil

1 head garlic, peeled of outer papery coats and cut in half

10 bay leaves

**Chile Oil:** *Sauté meat, poultry, fish, and vegetables in a little bit of this oil to add a terrific garlicky, spicy flavor to any recipe.*

**Makes about 2 cups.**

Gently heat all the ingredients together to 160°F in a double boiler. Keep warm 2 hours. Purée in a food processor, strain, and store in an airtight container at room temperature.

# Grilled Sole with Lime

*This dish is spicy! But like almost all Mexican dishes made with chiles, the heat is balanced, in this case by a copious amount of lime and cilantro. The fragrant green sauce provides the perfect counterpoint to the delicate texture and flavor of the fish. There are many kinds of soles, flounders, and dabs in North American waters. Some varieties are soft textured, even mushy. The best, like rex sole, mimic the firm, almost rubbery character of Dover sole. Regardless of the kind of sole you use, you may find it easier to grill the fillets in a grilling basket in order to keep them whole. Serve with Rice with Mint (page 104) and Refried Black Beans with Plantains (page 107).*

**Serves 4.**

Light the grill. Place a griddle or large cast-iron skillet over medium-hot fire to preheat. When very hot, brush fish with oil and season generously with salt and pepper. Cook sole until charred brown and just cooked through, about 10 minutes. A few minutes before fish is done, pour lime juice over fish. Remove to a serving platter and pour salsa over. Garnish with cilantro.

**4 rex sole fillets (about ¾ pound) or other flatfish fillets**

**2 tablespoons olive oil**

**Salt and freshly ground black pepper to taste**

**¼ cup freshly squeezed lime juice**

**Tomatillo Salsa (page 46)**

**¼ cup fresh cilantro leaves**

## Sea Bass Steamed with Hierba Santa

**4 to 6 fresh or dried *hierba santa* leaves, plus leaves for lining plate**

**1 whole sea bass (2 pounds) or 1 pound sea bass or halibut fillets**

**Salt and freshly ground black pepper**

**Authentic Guacamole (page 43)**

*This combination of mild, sweet sea bass and heady* hierba santa *is a real winner and very easy to make. Hierba santa, a large-leaved herb with an anise flavor, nicely complements the faintly aniselike flavor of avocado. To present this dish, unwrap the leaves so they form a plate liner displaying the white fish. Top the fillet with a dollop of guacamole and serve with fresh tortillas.*

**Serves 2.**

Light the grill and let burn down to a medium fire. If the *hierba santa* leaves are dried, reconstitute by soaking in warm water a few minutes. Squeeze out excess water, then carefully stretch out again to full size. Liberally season fish with salt and pepper. Lay a large sheet of aluminum foil on a countertop and arrange 2 or 3 *hierba santa* leaves in the center. Top with fish, then another 2 or 3 leaves. Seal foil around fish and grill until cooked through, about 15 minutes. A clue to knowing when the fish is done is to check along the seams of the foil for escaping, boiling juices. Serve with *hierba santa* leaves as a plate liner and guacamole on top of the fish.

## Grilled Squid Yucatán Style with Pineapple Salsa

**1 pound squid, cleaned**

**Bamboo skewers, soaked in water, or metal skewers**

**½ cup Traditional or Quick Achiote Recado (page 28)**

**Oil for grill**

**Grilled Pineapple Salsa (page 45)**

*Many people don't think of fresh ingredients, simply prepared, when they think of Mexican food. But this dish is exactly that. Thread some cleaned squid on a skewer, slather with a little achiote, and grill your salsa at the same time as the squid. If you already have your marinade and buy your squid cleaned, this is an easy dish. Try it with a nice, cold beer. Grill over a hot fire; charring tenderizes the squid. Serve with fresh tortillas.*

**Serves 2 or 3.**

Light the grill. Thread squid bodies on skewers in such a way as to keep bodies flat: Thread 1 skewer through the tip of several bodies and another skewer through the base of the bodies. Thread tentacles on another skewer. Brush squid liberally with *recado*. Oil grill and place squid over a very hot fire. Grill until crusty and deep brown on both sides, about 4 minutes. Serve with salsa.

# Grilled Salmon in Corn Husks

*I first saw fish grilled in corn husks in the Mercado Merced in Mexico City. These were tiny tadpoles and they smelled wonderful. Although I often eat in markets in Mexico, I did not want to chance eating anything from the highly polluted lake in Mexico City. When I returned to this country, I tried this dish with salmon. Salmon can lose its fresh, clean flavor when cooked directly over a too-hot fire, but the corn husks protect it and the flavor of corn is a perfect match with salmon.*

**Serves 2.**

Light the grill. Husk the corn, saving the largest outer leaves for wrapping the salmon. Grill corn over a hot fire, turning frequently, until brown (not black) all over, about 6 minutes. When corn is cool enough to handle, cut kernels from cobs and place in a small bowl. In another bowl, mix Chipotle Rub into the butter.

Lay 5 or 6 overlapping pieces of corn husk on a countertop. Arrange a piece of salmon in the center with one-fourth of the corn and one-fourth of the butter mixture. Scatter over some epazote and scallion. Fold over sides, top and bottom, to enclose fish, and tie with narrow strips torn from more corn husks. Don't be a perfectionist about this. Fish does not need to be fully enclosed, but do try and give a solid bottom to the packages to lessen leaking. Repeat to make 4 packages in all.

Place packages to one side of a hot fire, cover grill, and cook until corn husks are charred and salmon is cooked, about 8 minutes. Packages will open as they cook and butter will melt and might cause flare-ups. Serve 2 packages per person as a main course. Let them open the packages at the table. Serve salsa on the side.

**2 large ears of corn**

**1½ teaspoons Chipotle Rub (page 31)**

**8 tablespoons (1 stick) unsalted butter, softened**

**¾ pound salmon fillet, cut into 4 pieces, each about 1½ by 4 by ½ inch**

**4 fresh epazote leaves, chopped**

**1 tablespoon thinly sliced scallion, white and green parts**

**Tomatillo Salsa (page 46)**

# poultry

# Nothing benefits

from the Mexican grill more than poultry. Bland chicken treated with Chipotle Rub and served with Pico de Gallo salsa is transformed into a richly flavored confirmation of the pleasures of the Mexican table. All of the *recados* work well with poultry. The hardest part of mastering poultry on the grill is technique. We have all had the experience of eating badly grilled chicken—coated with a sticky sauce, charred black on the outside, and still raw near the bone. I have given a detailed description of my method for grilling poultry in the Techniques section. In addition, each individual recipe will also guide you to success.

In this chapter, I discuss four methods for grilling half chickens. Each demonstrates a different approach to creating perfect grilled chicken with crisp, spicy skin and juicy meat. I also discuss recipes for four brochettes, each perfect for an appetizer or light meal. There are more complex dishes as well—Grilled Duck with Pumpkin Seed Recado, Chicken Wrapped in Banana Leaves, Quail with Cinnamon and Mushroom Paella—that are sure to please the most adventuresome cook.

# Chicken Brochettes with Chipotle and Guacamole

*Little skewers of spicy meats with salsas make perfect appetizers or cocktail food. The blandness of boneless, skinless chicken breasts is a wonderful canvas for the assertive flavors of recados. Try the following brochette recipes together, serving them all at the same time, or serve just one, but with two or three salsas. Have a great party.*

**Serves 2 to 4.**

Lay the chicken on a countertop between sheets of waxed paper and pound lightly with a mallet until meat is an even ¼ inch thick. Cut diagonally into even strips about 1½ inches wide. Thread a single chicken piece lengthwise on each skewer. Brush both sides with oil and sprinkle with Chipotle Rub. Cover, refrigerate, and let marinate at least 1 hour or up to overnight.

    Light the grill and let burn down to a medium fire. Oil grill, then cook chicken, turning frequently, until brown and crusty, about 6 minutes. Be careful not to overcook or meat will be dry. Serve brochettes on a hot dish with a bowl of guacamole nearby for dipping. Garnish platter with cilantro sprigs.

**Variation with *Hierba Santa* and Avocado Árbol Salsa:** This dish was inspired by a Japanese yakitori dish of seasoned chicken wrapped in shiso leaf and grilled. Marinate chicken in 2 teaspoons olive oil and 2 teaspoons Garlic Rub (page 29). When ready to cook, wrap each skewer in a fresh or dried, rehydrated *hierba santa* leaf and thread on skewers. Brush with oil and grill as directed above. Be careful not to let herb burn. To serve, pull off most of leaf, especially charred bits. Serve with Avocado Árbol Salsa (page 44).

**Variation with Achiote and Grilled Pineapple Salsa:** Marinate chicken in 2 teaspoons olive oil and ½ cup Traditional or Quick Achiote Recado (page 28) at least 2 hours. Grill as directed above. Serve with Grilled Pineapple Salsa (page 45) and garnish with cilantro leaves and lime wedges.

**Variation with Pumpkin Seed Recado and Fragrant Salsa:** Marinate chicken in 2 teaspoons olive oil and ½ cup Pumpkin Seed Recado (page 32). Grill as directed above. Serve with Fragrant Salsa (page 44) and/or Pumpkin Seed Salsa (page 42). Garnish with diced radish and avocado slices.

1 whole skinless, boneless chicken breast (about ¾ pound)

2 teaspoons olive oil, plus more for oiling grill

2 teaspoons Chipotle Rub (page 31)

Bamboo skewers, soaked in water

Authentic Guacamole (page 43)

Fresh cilantro sprigs for garnish

# Grilled Half Chickens

*That a grilled half chicken is one of life's greatest pleasures is undeniable. My friend Jonathan Waxman used to sell a fabulous grilled half chicken with french fries at his New York restaurant, Jams. But unless you have a grill cook as good as Jonathan tending the fire, grilling chicken, particularly on the bone, is tricky. Add easily burned marinades like an achiote or adobo* recado, *and it is doubly tricky. Here are four methods for producing perfect grilled chicken in the Mexican style.*

4 half chickens (each about 1¼ pounds)

2 cups Adobo Recado (page 33)

Salt to taste

Oil for grill

**Chicken Marinated, Baked, then Grilled:** This method may sound like a lot of work, but it can be done ahead of time except for the final grilling, so you do not have to worry about getting perfect grilled chicken to your guests before hunger makes them rebel. Serve the chicken with Pico de Gallo (page 41), Authentic Guacamole (page 43), Black Beans with Nopales (page 108), and fresh, hot tortillas.

**Serves 4.**

Combine the chicken and *recado* in a large, nonreactive container or food storage bag and toss to coat well. Cover, refrigerate, and let marinate at least 4 hours or up to overnight. Turn occasionally to allow poultry to marinate evenly.

Preheat oven to 250°F. Remove chicken from marinade, shake off excess, and arrange, skin side up, in a single layer on a baking sheet. Bake until juices run clear, about 40 minutes. Remove chicken from oven and let cool to room temperature. (The recipe may be completed to this point 1 day ahead. Wrap well and refrigerate.)

Light the grill and let burn down to a slow fire. Season chicken generously with salt. Oil grill and arrange chicken, skin side down, on grill to side of fire. Cook chicken, turning frequently, until skin is brown and crisp, about 15 minutes. The marinade burns easily but do not fret. A little burned adobo tastes good. For most of cooking time, chicken should be skin side down on grill; this makes for crispier, lower-fat skin. To serve, cut through joints into serving pieces, if desired.

**Just Grilled Chicken:** This is either the easiest or hardest way to produce a perfectly grilled half chicken. If you are a confident grill cook, by all means, give it a try. The secret is the temperature of the fire. It should be hot enough to crisp the skin and render its fat, but not so that it burns. If grilling chicken well has so far escaped your best efforts, try the previous two methods. Which do I prefer? Each has a different taste and is outstanding in its own right. Serve this chicken with Norteño-Style Árbol Chile Salsa (page 38), Drunken Beans (page 104), and lots of fresh tortillas.

**Serves 4.**

Combine the chicken, ¼ cup olive oil, and Chipotle Rub in a large, nonreactive container or food storage bag and toss to coat well. Cover, refrigerate, and let marinate at least 1 hour or up to overnight.

Light the grill and let burn down to a slow fire. Oil grill. Place chicken, skin side down, on grill to side of fire. Cook slowly, moving pieces but not turning them, until skin begins to color. Turn and cook a few minutes backbone side down, then turn again. Keep turning chicken, skin side up and skin side down, backbone toward the fire, then away from the fire, so chicken cooks evenly and slowly. If chicken begin to cook too quickly, lay cover loosely on grill. Cook until fat renders and skin is brown and crisp, about 40 minutes. Turn chicken skin side down for 3 minutes to let it recrisp. Be careful not to overcook.

During the last few minutes of cooking, brush scallions with oil, season with salt and pepper, and place on grill. Cook slowly until marked by grill and soft, about 5 minutes. To serve chicken, cut through joints into serving pieces, if desired. Pile on platter with grilled scallions, and garnish with lime wedges, cilantro sprigs, and chopped radish.

**Chicken Marinated, Poached, then Grilled à la Plancha:** Second in our quest for perfect grilled chicken is an unusual method based on a terrific dish from Oaxaca, *pollo con oregano*. In the classic version of the dish, the chicken is first poached, then fried. What I have done here captures some of the essential flavor of that dish, while adding the wonderful perfume of the grill. Serve with Charred Tomato Mint Salsa (page 37), Authentic Guacamole (page 43), Oaxacan-Style Black Beans with Avocado Leaves (page 106), and plenty of fresh, hot tortillas.

**Serves 4.**

Combine the chicken and Garlic Rub in a large, nonreactive container or food storage bag and toss to coat well. Cover, refrigerate, and let marinate at least 1 hour or up to overnight. Purée garlic and 1 cup water in a blender

---

4 half chickens (each about 1¼ pounds)

¼ cup olive oil, plus more for oiling grill and brushing scallions

4⅓ cup Chipotle Rub (page 31)

1 bunch scallions, trimmed

Salt and freshly ground black pepper to taste

Lime wedges, cilantro sprigs, and chopped radish for garnish

---

4 half chickens (each about 1¼ pounds)

½ cup Garlic Rub (page 29)

1 head garlic, separated into cloves, pan-roasted until brown and soft, then peeled

1 cup water

¼ cup dried Mexican oregano

Oil for grill

until smooth. Pour into a large pot and add chicken and oregano. Add water to cover and place over medium heat. Bring just to below a simmer and cook until chicken registers 155°F on a meat thermometer, about 40 minutes from when heat was turned on.

Remove chicken and let cool, skin side up, on a rack. (The recipe may be completed to this point a day ahead. Wrap chicken well and refrigerate.)

Light the grill and let burn down to a slow fire. Oil grill and arrange chicken, skin side down, on grill to side of fire. Cook chicken, turning frequently, until fat renders and skin is brown and crisp, about 15 minutes. For most of cooking time, chicken should be skin side down on grill; this makes for crispier skin. To serve, cut through joints into serving pieces, if desired.

**4 half chickens (each about 1¼ pounds)**

**2 cups Traditional or Quick Achiote Recado (page 28)**

**Oil for grill**

**Glass-Skinned Chicken:** I discovered this method of cooking chicken quite by accident, or really, a series of accidents. I held some chickens on a warming shelf above the grill for about an hour before I crisped the skins to finish them. When I did, the skin was as light and crispy as that on a Peking duck. The beauty of grilling this way is really crispy skin and moist flesh. You could probably leave the chicken on the grill up to an hour without drying it out if the fire is low enough. Cooking at this low heat preserves moisture. Serve with Charred Habanero Salsa (page 39), Rajas made without cream or cheese, (page 109), Authentic Guacamole (page 43), and plenty of fresh, hot tortillas.

**Serves 4.**

Combine the chicken and *recado* in a large, nonreactive container or food storage bag and toss to coat well. Cover, refrigerate, and let marinate at least 4 hours or up to overnight. Turn occasionally to allow poultry to marinate evenly.

Preheat oven to 250°F. Remove chicken from marinade and shake off excess. Arrange, skin side up, in a single layer on a baking sheet. Place in oven and bake until cooked through, about 40 minutes. Let cool to room temperature. Recipe may be completed a day ahead to this point. Wrap well and refrigerate.

Light the grill and let burn down to a slow fire. Oil grill. Place chicken, skin side down, on grill to one side of the fire. Let cook very slowly until fat renders and skin crisps, about 30 minutes. Turn bone side down occasionally, especially if skin begins to overheat and color too fast. Skin will be a little burned in places and almost transparent, red, and fragile in others. The marinade burns easily. Do not be discouraged. A little burned achiote tastes good.

**8 to 10 boneless chicken thighs, skin on (about 2 pounds)**

**¼ cup olive oil, plus more for oiling grill**

**1 cup Traditional or Quick Achiote Recado (page 28)**

**1 nopal, spines removed**

**Pickled Onions (page 99)**

**Charred Habanero Salsa (page 39)**

**Authentic Guacamole (page 43)**

# Chicken in a Molcajete

*This is really a variation on some of the other grilled chicken dishes. The big difference is that here boneless thigh meat is used. This underappreciated meat is great for the grill because it is moister and more full-flavored than light white meat. So what is a* molcajete? *It is what I like to call my pre-Hispanic food processor, a lava-rock mortar that is the perfect tool for making salsas. It also makes an excellent, large serving dish to place in the center of the table. Serve with Drunken Beans (page 104) and tortillas.*

**Serves 4 or 5.**

Combine the chicken, ¼ cup olive oil, and achiote in a large nonreactive container or food storage bag and toss to coat well. Cover, refrigerate, and let marinate at least 4 hours or overnight.

Light the grill and let burn down to a medium fire. Oil grill. Remove chicken from marinade and shake off excess. Place, skin side down, on grill to one side of the fire, and cook slowly, moving pieces but not turning them, until skin begins to brown. Turn and continue to cook, turning frequently now, until juices run clear, about 20 minutes. Turn chicken, skin side down again, for 3 minutes to let recrisp.

During last 10 minutes of cooking, lay nopal leaf on grill with chicken and grill until soft and browned on both sides. When all is cooked, remove to a board. Cut the chicken and nopal leaf into 1-inch pieces and pile in a *molcajete* or serving bowl. Top with a handful of pickled onions and spoon some salsa over the top.

# Spicy Chicken Fajitas

*It makes me happy that this quirky dish is now such a mainstay that McDonald's serves something called by the same name. I feel this is proof that the United States is finally paying attention to Mexico and Mexican food. Ironically, this dish is not Mexican at all but a ranch-hand border specialty of south Texas. It is classically made with skirt steak, a formerly cheap cut now made fashionable and expensive by this dish. At taquerias in the Latin parts of town and in Mexico, you will find a dish very like fajitas called* tacos al carbon *(grilled meat tacos). You may use skinless chicken here, if you wish, but the flavor will suffer. Make a lot and invite your friends. Serve with Pico de Gallo (page 41), Authentic Guacamole (page 43), Drunken Beans (page 104), and fresh, hot tortillas. And in this instance, tortillas mean flour, not corn, tortillas, since this is a south Texas dish.*

**Serves 4 to 6.**

Combine the chicken, olive oil, Chipotle Rub, beer, and lime juice in a large, nonreactive container or food storage bag and toss to coat well. Cover, refrigerate, and let marinate at least 2 hours or up to overnight.

Light the grill and let burn down to a slow fire. Oil grill. Remove chicken from marinade and shake off excess. Place, skin side down, on grill and cook slowly, moving pieces but not turning them, until fat is rendered and skin begins to brown. Turn and continue to cook, turning frequently now, until juices run clear and pieces are firm to the touch, about 10 minutes for breasts and 15 minutes for thighs. Turn chicken, skin side down again, for 3 minutes to recrisp.

Cut into ½-inch-wide strips and serve on a warm metal or ceramic platter with warm Rajas poured over the top. Garnish with lime wedges and cilantro sprigs.

**2 pounds boneless chicken breasts or thighs, or a mixture**

**¼ cup olive oil, plus more for oiling grill**

**¼ cup Chipotle Rub (page 31)**

**½ cup dark Mexican beer such as Negra Modelo**

**Juice of 1 lime**

**Rajas made without cream or cheese, (page 109)**

# Chicken Wrapped in Banana Leaves

6 to 8 half chicken breasts, skinned and trimmed of fat (about 2 pounds)

¼ cup olive oil

2 cups Traditional or Quick Achiote Recado (page 28)

2 pieces banana leaves, 12 by 24 inches each

6 fresh epazote leaves (optional)

Pollo pibil, *chicken wrapped in banana leaves with achiote and cooked in a earthen pit, is one of the classics of Yucatán cuisine. The technique is a complicated one: It involves digging a shallow, broad hole, piling some rocks in it, burning a fire on the rocks until the fire burns down and the rocks are hot, putting the seasoned chicken and garnishes on the rocks, covering them with leaves or burlap, then a layer of dirt, and finally, burning another fire on top. The result is fabulous, but a lot of work. If you want to try a nearly authentic alternative, try this grill-top method. Serve with a dish of sliced habanero chiles in orange juice and a little lemon juice, Charred Habanero Salsa (page 39), Pickled Onions (page 99), Oaxacan-Style Black Beans with Avocado Leaves (page 106), and fresh, hot tortillas.*

**Serves 4 to 6.**

Combine the chicken, olive oil, and *recado* in a large, nonreactive container or food storage bag and toss to coat well. Cover, refrigerate, and let marinate at least 4 hours or up to overnight.

Light the grill and let burn down to a medium fire. Wash banana leaves well in hot water and toast briefly by holding over an open flame until fragrant, about 1 minute total. Lay a large sheet of heavy-duty aluminum foil on a countertop. Lay banana leaves in a cross on top. Pile chicken in center of crossed leaves and, if using, top with epazote. Fold leaves over and around chicken to form a bundle, then wrap foil around leaves to make a neat package. Place on grill, seam side up, to one side of fire. Cover grill and let cook about 30 minutes. Open foil slightly to allow some smoke flavor to penetrate, cover grill again, and continue to cook until chicken is cooked through, about 20 minutes more. Remove bundle from grill and place on heated serving dish. Unwrap at the table. The aroma will make you a star.

# Chicken Broth

*Since the broth will not be reduced and the chicken is to be used later, we add salt. This also helps to keep it longer.*

**Makes about 8 cups.**

Put all the ingredients in a large pot. Add 8 cups cold water to cover and put a plate on top of the chicken to keep it submerged. Do not cover pot. Bring slowly to a simmer over medium heat; this may take about 45 minutes. Cook until a meat thermometer inserted into chicken reads 150°F, about 1 hour.

Remove from heat and let chicken cool in the broth, then remove chicken and refrigerate for later use (shred for enchiladas, salad, and so on). Strain the broth into a large container and refrigerate, covered, until fat rises to top and solidifies. Discard fat and return to refrigerator up to 5 days, or freeze up to 2 months.

**1 chicken (3 to 4 pounds)**

**1 white onion, thickly sliced and pan-roasted until brown and soft**

**4 cloves garlic, pan-roasted until brown and soft, then peeled**

**2 carrots, peeled and sliced**

**1 teaspoon dried Mexican oregano**

**10 whole allspice**

**3 whole cloves**

**1 tablespoon whole black peppercorns**

**4 fresh flat-leaf parsley sprigs**

**1 tablespoon kosher salt**

# Spicy Quail with Green Chorizo

*I love quail. I love sausage, too. Green chorizo—pork sausage flavored with pumpkin seeds, epazote, and jalapeño—is the perfect partner to crisp grilled quail. I like to serve them together resting on top of a brothy bowl of beans. This is real soul food to me.*

**Serves 4.**

Light the grill and let burn down to a medium fire. Put the quail, Chipotle Rub, and olive oil in a nonreactive bowl and toss to coat well. Let marinate about 30 minutes.

Oil grill and place quail, skin side down, on grill with sausages. Grill quail, turning once, until brown and crispy and cooked to medium doneness, about 5 minutes. Cook sausages, turning so they brown all over, until cooked through, about 10 minutes. Divide hot beans among 4 large soup bowls. Arrange a quail and a sausage patty on top of each bowl. Serve with salsa and sprinkle with radish.

**4 quail (about ¼ pound each), butterflied**

**2 teaspoons Chipotle Rub (page 31)**

**2 teaspoons olive oil, plus more for oiling grill**

**1 pound green chorizo, stuffed into casings or shaped into 3-inch diameter patties (page 90)**

**Drunken Beans (page 104), heated**

**Pico de Gallo (page 41)**

**⅓ cup chopped radish**

2 whole cloves

6 whole allspice

1 piece cinnamon stick (1 inch long), preferably Mexican, broken

15 whole black peppercorns

8 quail (about ¼ pound each), butterflied or halved lengthwise

2 tablespoons Mexican or Spanish brandy

4 teaspoons Garlic Rub (page 29)

6 cups Chicken Broth (page 77)

6 tablespoons olive oil

1 medium-sized white onion, diced

2 tablespoons dried currants

1 bay leaf

3 ounces dry-cured ham, such as Smithfield or Spanish serrano, diced

1 clove garlic, minced

3 Roma (plum) tomatoes, pan-roasted until blistered, deeply browned, and soft

Large pinch of saffron threads

1 cup fresh wild mushrooms, such as halved morels, or sliced domestic mushrooms

1½ cups short-grain rice such as Arborio

2 tablespoons finely chopped fresh flat-leaf parsley

1 teaspoon kosher salt

# Quail with Cinnamon and Mushroom Paella

*This dish is more Spanish than Mexican in inspiration, but it is often hard to separate the strands of these two cuisines. The spicing is typically Mexican, except the saffron, which speaks of Moorish influences in Spain. Mexican cinnamon is different from the cinnamon we commonly use. Ours smells like apple pie, while Mexican cinnamon tastes like Red Hots candies. Take the time to search it out in Mexican and Latin American groceries. This is fabulous party fare. The entire dish can be prepared on the grill.*

**Serves 4 to 6.**

In a spice mill, grind together the cloves, allspice, cinnamon stick, and peppercorns to a fine powder. Place the quail in a large, nonreactive bowl and pour over brandy, 2 teaspoons of the spice mix, and the Garlic Rub. Toss well and let marinate about 30 minutes. (Keep leftover spice mixture in a tightly covered jar for flavoring soups, stews, sausage, and chicken.)

Light the grill and let burn down to a medium fire. Heat stock to just below a simmer in a large pot. Place a paella pan or large, shallow sauté pan on grill and add the olive oil. When hot, add the onion, currants, bay leaf, ham, and garlic and sauté until translucent, about 10 minutes. Add another ½ teaspoon spice mix to pan with tomatoes, saffron, and mushrooms and sauté 5 minutes. Add the rice and parsley and sauté until rice is translucent, about 5 minutes more. Add the salt and 1½ cups of the broth, stir well, and let come to a simmer. Broth should just cover rice. Cook until broth is absorbed; do not stir. Add more broth only when previous addition has been completely absorbed. Cook until rice is done and has absorbed all the broth. If rice is not fully cooked, add water and continue to cook until it is. It should take about 25 minutes. Keep the pan to one side of the fire at a simmer, shifting pan from side to side, to allow even cooking. When rice is done, move pan to center of fire for a few minutes to give the bottom layer of rice a little crust. (This is the best part!)

A few minutes before rice is done, grill the quail, skin side down, until brown and crispy, then turn and cook until medium doneness, about 5 minutes. To serve, pile the quail in center of the rice and carry directly to the table.

# Grilled Duck with Pumpkin Seed Recado

*One of the classic dishes of Mexican haute cuisine is duck in a pumpkin seed sauce. The richness of duck is a wonderful counterpoint to the nuttiness of the seeds. This dish makes use of pumpkin seeds twice: in the recado* for grilling the duck and again in the salsa to serve with the finished dish.

**Serves 4.**

Score skin side of duck breasts in several places. Place them, skin side down, in a cold sauté pan and put over low heat. Slowly render fat from breasts, about 10 minutes. Remove duck breasts to a plate; pour fat into a jar and reserve. Pat about 2 tablespoons of the *recado* onto the flesh side of each breast, forming a thick layer. Cover, refrigerate, and let marinate overnight.

When ready to cook, preheat oven to 400°F. In a small baking dish, toss together pumpkin, 1 tablespoon of the duck fat, onion, and ½ teaspoon salt. (Reserve remaining duck fat for another use.) Cover tightly and place in oven. Bake until very soft, about 45 minutes. Purée in a food processor, taste for seasoning, then scrape into a warmed serving bowl. Keep warm.

Light the grill and let burn down to a medium fire. Lightly season duck on skin side with salt and pepper. Oil grill. Start to grill duck, skin side down, then turn and cook second side. Take care when turning that the *recado* does not fall off into the fire. Duck should be done to medium-rare in about 5 minutes.

To serve, place duck on top of pumpkin purée and top with a spoonful of salsa. Serve more salsa at the table.

**4 large, boneless duck breasts (about 2 pounds each), skin on**

**Pumpkin Seed Recado (page 32)**

**1 pound pumpkin or butternut squash, peeled, seeded, and cut into ½-inch-thick pieces**

**1 small white onion, minced**

**Salt and freshly ground black pepper to taste**

**Oil for grill**

**Pumpkin Seed Salsa (page 42)**

## Duck and Pomegranate Tacos

**4 large boneless duck breasts (about 2 pounds each), skin on**

**Mint Recado (page 31)**

**1 cup pomegranate juice or cranberry juice, or ¼ cup pomegranate molasses mixed with ¾ cup water**

**Oil for grill**

**Small tortillas, heated**

**2 scallions, white and green parts, chopped**

**Charred Habanero Salsa (page 39)**

*Pomegranates are a Spanish import to Mexico, where people have taken to them because they are both sweet and brightly colored. This recipe uses one of my favorite treatments for game: a tenderizing and flavorful marinade of pomegranate juice and mint. It works well on venison and quail, and equally well on lamb and duck. When pomegranates are out of season, I have found that pomegranate molasses (available in Middle Eastern groceries) is a good substitute.*

**Serves 4.**

Score skin side of duck breasts in several places. Place them, skin side down, in a cold sauté pan and put over low heat. Slowly render fat from breasts, about 10 minutes. Remove duck breasts to a large, nonreactive bowl; pour fat into a jar and reserve for other uses. Add the *recado* and pomegranate or cranberry juice to duck and mix well. Cover, refrigerate, and let marinate overnight.

Light the grill and let burn down to a medium fire. Oil grill. Remove duck from marinade and shake off excess. Start to grill duck, skin side down, then turn and cook second side. Duck should be done to medium-rare in about 5 minutes. Do not overcook. Chop meat coarsely and wrap in tortillas with chopped scallions and salsa.

meats

# I don't think any

food is more popular in Mexico—or in the United States—than a piece of grilled meat. From street vendors selling tacos to cooks in *nueva cocina* restaurants, everyone seems to agree that grilling brings out something special in meats.

In this chapter, we start with a few simple, quick grills such as Pork in a *Molcajete* and Rib-Eye Steak with Green Chile Mushroom Salsa Butter. I have not forgotten to include beef fajitas; you may not want to eat another restaurant version once you try them with Chipotle Rub. I also use the grill to slow-cook dishes such as Lamb in Banana Leaves. First the lamb is marinated in adobo, then it is wrapped in banana leaves and cooked for hours on a covered grill until it almost melts. Although it may sound complex, it is actually very easy.

# Pork in Adobo

*Spicy red adobo was used before refrigeration to preserve meat. In Mexico and the American Southwest, pork is still cut into strips, rubbed with adobo, and hung up to dry like laundry. The resulting salty, gamy meat might be delicately described as an acquired taste. But as is often the case with very old recipes, updating the technique can transform the recipe into a delightful modern dish. The result is spicy, sweet, charred, and juicy pork—a little hog heaven that can only be improved by the addition of Tropical Fruit Salsa (page 45), Black Beans with Nopales (page 108), and fresh, hot tortillas.*

**Serves 4.**

Mix ½ cup of the *recado* and the water in a small bowl. Combine the pork and *recado* in a large, nonreactive container or food storage bag and toss to coat well. Cover, refrigerate, and let marinate overnight. Pork will keep up to 5 days at this point, but will get saltier with time.

Light the grill. Drain pork and pat dry with paper towels. Brush pork with remaining ½ cup *recado*. Oil grill and cook pork over a very hot fire until charred and just cooked through, about 8 minutes. Be careful not to overcook, meat may continue to look pink even when overcooked because of the marinade.

**1 cup Adobo Recado (page 33)**

**1 cup water**

**8 thin pork loin chops, with tenderloin attached (about 2 pounds)**

**Oil for grill**

# Pork in a Molcajete

1½ pounds trimmed pork tenderloin, cut into 2-by-4-by-¼-inch strips

1 cup Achiote Recado (page 28)

Olive oil for grill, plus 1 tablespoon

4 small nopales, spines removed

2 bunches scallions, trimmed

1½ teaspoons Garlic Rub (page 29), or salt and freshly ground black pepper to taste

½ pound queso fresco, farmer cheese, sheep's milk feta, or fresh goat cheese, cut into pieces

*I first had meat served in a* molcajete *(the traditional Mexican mortar) in a little taqueria in Mexico City. I was so captivated with the presentation that I put this dish on the menu at the (now defunct) Corona Bar & Grill in San Francisco. If you don't have a* molcajete, *try using a plate covered with a banana leaf. Serve with Charred Habanero Salsa (page 39), Drunken Beans (page 104), and fresh, hot tortillas.*

**Serves 4.**

Combine the pork and *recado* in a medium-sized, nonreactive container or food storage bag and toss to coat well. Cover, refrigerate, and let marinate overnight. Pork will keep up to 5 days at this point, but meat will get saltier with time.

Light the grill. Drain pork and shake off excess marinade. Oil grill and cook pork over a very hot fire until charred and just cooked through, about 3 minutes. Be careful not to overcook; meat will continue to look pink even when overcooked because of the marinade. Meanwhile, lightly oil nopales and scallions and season with Garlic Rub or salt and pepper. Grill until soft and browned on both sides, about 10 minutes for nopales and 5 minutes for scallions.

To serve, coarsely chop pork strips and serve in a warmed *molcajete*. Arrange nopales, scallions, and cheese alongside.

# Pork in Banana Leaves

*Your grill will do much more than just grill. If you have a kettle-type barbecue at home, try this astoundingly good variation on the classic* cochinita pibil *(pork cooked in a pit). Make this dish for a backyard party and feed a crowd. It's as easy to cook enough for ten as to make a single portion. Carefully wrapped leftovers are wonderful reheated. You'll need to plan ahead, however, as the pork must marinate for at least two days. Serve with the simple salsa included in the recipe below and one or more of others in this book. I recommend Charred Tomato Mint Salsa (page 37), Charred Habanero Salsa (page 39), or Tropical Fruit Salsa (page 45). Whatever salsa you choose, don't forget Refried Black Beans with Plantains (page 107) and fresh, hot tortillas.*

**Serves 6 to 8.**

Combine the meat and *recado* in a large, nonreactive container or food storage bag and toss to coat well, cover, refrigerate, and let marinate 2 days. Pork will keep up to 5 days at this point, but meat will get saltier with time.

Light the grill and let burn down to a slow fire. Drain the pork, reserving marinade. Lay a large sheet of heavy-duty aluminum foil on a countertop. Wash banana leaves well in hot water. Cross banana leaves on top and pile pork in center. Pour reserved marinade over pork. It is important that the pork stew in the marinade. Wrap leaves around meat, then wrap foil around leaves to make a neat package. Place on grill, seam side up, to one side of the fire. Cover grill and cook until fork tender, about 4 hours. About halfway through cooking, crack open foil to allow smoke flavors to penetrate. Add more charcoal as necessary to maintain fire.

Mix chiles with orange and lemon juices in a small, nonreactive bowl and set aside at least 30 minutes before serving. When pork is done, pour contents of package into a large bowl and coarsely shred pork, removing any fatty pieces. The pork will have absorbed most of the achiote. Serve on a warmed platter topped with Pickled Onions and with the orange juice—habanero salsa on the side.

**3 pounds boned pork shoulder or butt roast, cut into 2-inch-thick slices (with fat)**

**Double recipe Traditional or Quick Achiote Recado (page 28)**

**2 pieces banana leaf, each 12 by 24 inches**

**4 habanero chiles with seeds, thinly sliced**

**1 cup freshly squeezed orange juice**

**¼ cup freshly squeezed lemon juice**

**Pickled Onions (page 99)**

# Pork Ribs with Tamarind Recado

2 slabs baby back pork ribs (about 1 pound each)

¼ cup Chipotle Rub (page 31)

Tamarind Recado (page 29)

Oil for grill

Charred Tomato Mint Salsa (page 37)

*I love ribs. There is an old saying in the South: "The closer to the bone, the sweeter the meat." Nothing could be sweeter than great ribs. I think this recipe makes some of the best ribs you'll ever eat. Note that it takes a couple of days to marinate the meat. Serve with Grilled Corn on the Cob with Chipotle Rub and Lime (page 102).*

**Serves 4 to 6.**

Two days before you plan to cook, rub ribs with Chipotle Rub. Place in a large, nonreactive container or food storage bag, cover, refrigerate, and let marinate overnight. The next day, add the *recado* and toss to coat well. Recover and refrigerate until ready to use. Pork will keep up to 5 days at this point, but meat will get saltier with time.

Light the grill and let burn down to a slow fire. Remove pork from tamarind marinade, shaking off excess and reserving marinade. Oil grill and place ribs, bone side down, on grill. Cover and cook until tamarind sets and dries a bit, about 10 minutes. Turn, baste, and continue to cook, covered, another 10 minutes. Uncover grill and continue to cook, basting often with reserved marinade, until crusty and brown on both sides, another 10 to 20 minutes. Do not baste the last 5 minutes of cooking.

To serve, slice meat between ribs and arrange on platter with salsa.

## Chipotle, Garlic, or Green Chorizo

*These are three simple, fresh sausages with exotic flavors imparted by the* recados *used to season them. The sausages are fairly lean because the natural marbling of the pork is the only fat. Serve them on their own, as part of a mixed grill, or for breakfast with soft scrambled eggs, hot tortillas, and salsa. Recipes may be easily doubled or halved, depending on your need and appetite.*

**Each recipe makes four ¼-pound patties.**

Select one of the recipes and put the ingredients in a medium-sized bowl. Knead lightly to mix well. Form into patties 3 inches in diameter or stuff into casings. Cover and refrigerate a few hours or overnight before using to let flavors develop. (Do not keep longer than 3 days.)

Light the grill and let burn down to a medium fire. Oil grill and cook sausages until crusty and brown on both sides, about 5 minutes.

**Chipotle Chorizo**
1 pound coarsely ground pork shoulder

1½ tablespoons dark Mexican Beer such as Negra Modelo

1 tablespoon plus 1 teaspoon Chipotle Rub (page 31)

**Garlic Chorizo**
1 pound coarsely ground pork shoulder

½ tablespoon Garlic Rub (page 29)

¼ cup Adobo Recado (page 33)

**Green Chorizo**
1 pound coarsely ground pork shoulder

⅓ cup Pumpkin Seed Recado (page 32)

2 fresh epazote leaves, chopped

1 tablespoon minced jalapeño with seeds

¾ teaspoon salt

## Lamb in a Molcajete

*Soft, rich cheese is a great foil for charred, red meats. With lamb, I prefer sheep's or goat's milk cheeses. Try a goat cheese with a little age, or a feta if it is not too salty. This is great party fare. Serve with Refried Black Beans with Plantains (page 107) and fresh, hot tortillas.*

**Serves 4.**

Combine the lamb and *recado* in a large, nonreactive container or food storage bag and toss to coat well. Cover, refrigerate, and let marinate about 2 hours. Do not marinate more than 2 days or meat will dry out.

Light the grill and let burn down to a medium-hot fire. Remove lamb from marinade and shake off excess. Oil grill and cook lamb until crusty and cooked medium-rare, turning as necessary, about 3 to 5 minutes. Meanwhile, lightly oil nopales and scallions and season with Garlic Rub

1½ pounds trimmed meat from leg of lamb, cut into 2-by-4-by-¼-inch strips

1 cup Tamarind Recado (page 29)

1 tablespoon olive oil, plus more for oiling grill

4 small nopales, spines removed

2 bunches scallions, trimmed

1½ teaspoons Garlic Rub (page 29), or salt and freshly ground black pepper to taste

Charred Tomato Mint Salsa (page 37)

¼ pound Bûcheron or other semi-dry goat cheese

1 tablespoon coarsely chopped fresh cilantro

or salt and pepper to taste. Grill until soft and browned on both sides, about 10 minutes for nopales and 5 minutes for scallions.

To serve, coarsely chop lamb strips and serve in a warmed *molcajete*. Arrange nopales and scallions alongside. Drizzle with salsa, crumble the cheese over the top, and sprinkle with cilantro.

## Leg of Lamb in Adobo

*Lamb is my favorite domesticated red meat. It retains a hint of gamy, grassy flavor because it is generally not feedlot fattened, but, instead, grazes on wild grasses. The flavor of lamb is enhanced by adobo and the smoky, charred grill flavor. While a whole leg of lamb is clearly party fare, most butchers will sell you a smaller piece of the leg that can be prepared the same way. Serve with Grilled Goat Cheese in Banana Leaves (page 102), Oaxacan-Style Black Beans with Avocado Leaves (page 106), and fresh, hot tortillas.*

**Serves 8.**

Meat should be butterflied to as even a 2-inch thickness as possible. Combine the meat and *recado* in a large, nonreactive container or food storage bag and toss to coat well. Cover, refrigerate, and let marinate overnight. Do not marinate more than 2 days or meat will dry out.

Light the grill and let burn down to a medium-show fire. Remove lamb from marinade and shake off excess. Oil grill and cook lamb until crusty and done (120°F on a meat thermometer for rare meat), turning as necessary, about 20 minutes. Let rest on a warm platter several minutes before carving. Meat should be pinkish red when you cut into it. Slice into thin slices across the grain. Garnish with lots of cilantro sprigs and drizzle with salsa.

**½ boned leg of lamb (3 to 4 pounds), butterflied**

**Adobo Recado (page 33)**

**Oil for grill**

**Fresh cilantro sprigs for garnish**

**Green Chile Mushroom Salsa (page 41)**

# Lamb in Banana Leaves

4 lamb shanks (each about 1 pound)

Double recipe Adobo Recado (page 33)

2 pieces banana leaf, 12 by 24 inches each

1 small white onion, finely chopped

1 small bunch fresh cilantro, coarsely chopped

*This is a variation on the classic lamb in maguey cactus from central Mexico. Called* barbacoa, *it is obviously a precursor of what we call barbecue. I think you will be surprised how good well done lamb can be and how much better a barbecue sauce adobo* recado *is than that bottled stuff. Serve with Pumpkin Seed Salsa (page 42), Fragrant Salsa (page 44), Oaxacan-Style Black Beans with Avocado Leaves (page 106), and fresh, hot tortillas.*

**Serves 4 to 6.**

Combine the lamb and *recado* in a large, nonreactive container or food storage bag and toss to coat well. Cover, refrigerate, and let marinate overnight. Do not let marinate more than 2 days or meat will dry out.

Light the grill and let burn down to a slow fire. Drain the lamb shanks, reserving the marinade. Lay a large sheet of heavy-duty aluminum foil on a countertop. Wash banana leaves well in hot water. Cross banana leaves on top and pile meat in center. Pour over as much of the reserved marinade as will fit. It is important that the meat stew in the marinade. Wrap leaves around lamb, then wrap foil around leaves to make a neat package. Place on grill, seam side up, to one side of the fire. Cover grill and cook until fork tender, about 4 hours. About halfway through cooking, crack open foil to allow smoke flavors to penetrate. Add more charcoal as necessary to maintain fire.

When done, pour contents of package into a medium-sized bowl and coarsely shred lamb, removing any fatty pieces. Lamb will have absorbed most of the marinade. Serve on a warmed platter topped with onion and cilantro.

# Beef in a Molcajete

*I first had pork served to me in a* molcajete *(the traditional Mexican "food processor") in a little place in Mexico City. Since then I've created all sorts of variations on the theme for different meats. This beef is both juicy and full of flavor.*

**Serves 4.**

Light the grill. Put beef in a large, nonreactive container or food storage bag, season with ¼ cup Garlic Rub, and moisten with beer. Let marinate briefly, up to 30 minutes, while grill heats.

Oil grill and cook beef over a very hot fire until crusty and still rare, turning as necessary, about 3 minutes. Meanwhile, lightly oil nopales and scallions and season with remaining 1½ teaspoons Garlic Rub or salt and pepper. Grill until soft and browned on both sides, about 10 minutes for nopales and 5 minutes for scallions.

To serve, coarsely chop beef strips and serve in a warmed *molcajete*. Drizzle with Green Chile Mushroom Salsa, arrange a circle of Pico de Gallo around the perimeter, and tuck nopales, scallions, and cheese alongside. Scatter cilantro across the top.

**1½ pounds trimmed beef tenderloin, cut into 2-by-4-by-1-inch strips**

**¼ cup plus 1½ teaspoons Garlic Rub (page 29)**

**¼ cup dark Mexican beer such as Negra Modelo**

**Oil for grill, plus 1 tablespoon**

**4 small nopales, spines removed**

**2 bunches scallions, trimmed**

**Salt and freshly ground black pepper to taste, if not using Garlic Rub**

**Green Chile Mushroom Salsa (page 41)**

**Pico de Gallo (page 41)**

**½ pound queso fresco, farmer cheese, goat cheese, or sheep's milk feta, cut into pieces**

**1 tablespoon coarsely chopped fresh cilantro**

# Rib-Eye Steak with Green Chile Mushroom Salsa Butter

*The rib of beef is my favorite cut. Some people don't like it because it often has little "eyes" of fat in the middle of the steaks. I just pop these out with my fingers or a knife before I grill the beef. This recipe yields a great charred, smoky steak with loads of spicy wild mushroom flavor to go along.*

**Serves 2.**

Light the grill. Brush the steaks on both sides with oil then season with Chipotle Rub. Let marinate briefly, up to 30 minutes, while grill heats.

Oil grill and cook steaks over a very hot fire, turning as necessary, until crusty and cooked rare to medium-rare, about 5 minutes. Let rest briefly on a warm platter.

To serve, arrange steaks on top of beans in a deep platter and let a large chunk of salsa butter melt over each steak. Top with a few onion rings.

**2 rib-eye steaks (8 to 10 ounces each)**

**1 tablespoon olive oil, plus more for oiling grill**

**4 teaspoons Chipotle Rub (page 31)**

**1½ cups Drunken Beans (page 104)**

**2 to 3 tablespoons Salsa Butter made from Green Chile Mushroom Salsa (page 47)**

**Chipotle Fried Onion Rings (page 100)**

# Spiced Skirt Steak Fajitas

2 pounds skirt steak, trimmed of fat and tough membranes

3 tablespoons Chipotle Rub (page 31)

1 small white onion, finely diced

½ cup dark Mexican beer such as Negra Modelo

½ cup plus 1 tablespoon olive oil, plus more for oiling grill

2 bunches scallions, trimmed

1 teaspoon Garlic Rub (page 29), or salt and freshly ground black pepper to taste

Fresh cilantro sprigs and lime wedges for garnish

*The first time I had fajitas was in a little joint near the produce market in San Antonio. It was 1976. I have now seen all sorts of strange dishes called fajitas served in all sorts of unlikely places. McDonald's. Paris. It is funny how a dish created by ranch hands in south Texas to use up a tasty but little-used cut of beef called skirt steak has become so popular. Indeed, the price of skirt steak has even tripled in the last six years. This is my (slight) variation on the original—a dish worth preserving before it vanishes into the soft, fuzzy standards of popular culture. Be sure to use mesquite wood to intensify the flavor of the grilled beef. Serve with Pico de Gallo salsa (page 41), Authentic Guacamole (page 43), Drunken Beans (page 104), and plenty of fresh, hot tortillas. Since this is a Texas border dish, the tortillas should be flour, not corn.*

**Serves 6 to 8.**

Light the grill. Put the steak on a nonreactive platter and sprinkle both sides with Chipolte Rub and onion, then moisten with beer and ½ cup olive oil. Let marinate briefly, up to 30 minutes, while grill heats.

Remove steak from marinade, shaking off excess, but retaining some onion on the meat when it grills. Oil grill and cook steak over a blazing hot fire, turning as necessary, until crusty and cooked medium-rare, about 3 minutes. (To be perfectly authentic, cook well done; cattlemen, as a rule, dislike rare beef.) Let rest a few minutes before carving. Meanwhile, brush scallions with oil and season with Garlic Rub or salt and pepper. Place on grill alongside meat and grill until browned and tender, about 5 minutes. Do not grill over too high a heat.

To serve, slice the steak into thin slices across the grain and pile on a warmed platter with the grilled scallions. Garnish with cilantro sprigs and lime wedges.

# Beef Sabana with Avocado Árbol Salsa

*The* sabana, *or "sheet," is a long, paper-thin strip cut from a beef tender-loin. In Mexico, the beef is salted and hung at room temperature until it is sold, resulting in a salty, gamy flavor. By changing the dish to fit contemporary tastes, the result is a thin, charred, spicy steak with an elegant and sophisticated Oaxacan salsa of avocado, árbol chile, and avocado leaf. Serve with Oaxacan-Style Black Beans with Avocado Leaves (page 106).*

**Serves 4.**

Light the grill. Cut the beef along the grain into 4 long, thin strips, each about ¼ inch thick. Brush both sides with the 1 tablespoon oil and sprinkle with Garlic Rub. Let marinate briefly, up to 30 minutes, while grill heats.

Oil grill and cook beef over a very hot fire, turning as necessary, until crusty and brown, 2 to 3 minutes. Beef should be cooked rare to medium-rare.

To serve, arrange meat on 4 warmed plates, drizzle with salsa, sprinkle with grilled mushrooms and queso fresco, and serve immediately.

**1½ pounds trimmed beef tenderloin, in 1 piece**

**1 tablespoon olive oil, plus more for oiling grill**

**2 teaspoons Garlic Rub (page 29)**

**Avocado Árbol Salsa (page 44)**

**Grilled Wild Mushrooms (page 103)**

**2 tablespoons crumbled queso fresco, farmer cheese, fresh goat cheese, or sheep's milk feta**

# vegetables

# Many fresh vegetables

have a lot of natural sugar. This sugar benefits from the process of caramelization that happens over an open grill. The sweetness in corn, for instance, is transformed into a nuttiness complemented by the smokiness of the grill and a spicy *recado*.

Beans are the ubiquitous partner to much of Mexican food. In this chapter, I give four of my favorite bean recipes, each typical of a different region. While vegetables do not play as obvious a role in this book as they do today in many people's dining habits, remember that the salsas and other accompaniments to the food are largely based on vegetables and grains. This is healthful, high-fiber, low-fat cooking at its flavorful best.

# Pickled Onions

*Here is a wonderful, crisp accompaniment to many of the dishes in this book. They are a snap to make and are pleasantly cooling on an unbearably hot day. Since the onions are most frequently scattered over hot poultry and meat, they should not be served ice cold. Remove them from the refrigerator in advance of when you need them, so that they come to room temperature. They are splendid for snacking and for sandwiches as well.*

**Serves 8 to 10.**

Put the cider, sugar, salt, clove, and allspice in a large, nonreactive saucepan, place over high heat, and bring to a boil. Put the onions in a large, nonreactive bowl and pour the boiling pickling liquid over them. Toss well and allow to sit, tossing occasionally, until cool. Onions will wilt and turn a pretty pink. Let sit 3 to 4 hours before using. Or cover and refrigerate for up to 5 days.

2 cups apple cider vinegar

½ cup sugar

2 teaspoons salt

1 whole clove

3 whole allspice

3 large red onions, very thinly sliced

# Grilled Onion and Pineapple

*Taquerias in Mexico almost all sell tacos al pastor, shepherd's-style tacos. Curiously enough, shepherds apparently eat pork, because these tacos are always made with pork marinated in adobo sauce. The meat is cooked on a little rotisserie just like the one Greeks use for gyros. An onion and a big chunk of pineapple are usually roasting along with the meat. They are delicious alongside grilled pork (or fish or chicken).*

**Serves 4.**

Light the grill and let burn down to a medium fire. Brush pineapple, onion, and jalapeño chile with oil. Grill until browned but not burned, about 10 minutes. Turn frequently. Be careful; pineapple has a lot of sugar in it and burns easily.

Coarsely chop pineapple and onion together and place in a bowl. Peel, seed, and devein chile, if desired, and add to pineapple-onion mixture. Use as a salsa or condiment.

4 slices pineapple (½ inch thick), peeled and cored

2 slices large white onion (½ inch thick)

1 jalapeño chile, seeds optional

2 tablespoons olive oil

Corn oil for deep-frying

½ cup all-purpose flour

2 teaspoons Chipotle Rub (page 31)

1 medium-sized white onion, very thinly sliced and separated into rings

1 small jalapeño chile with seeds, minced

¼ cup freshly squeezed lime juice

½ cup extra-virgin olive oil

⅛ teaspoon salt, plus salt to taste

½ clove garlic, minced

2 large ripe tomatoes (about 1¾ pounds), cut into large chunks

1 small sweet onion such as Bermuda or Vidalia, sliced ¼ inch thick and separated into rings

2 medium-sized, ripe avocados, peeled, pitted, and cut lengthwise into slices about ⅜ inch thick

Freshly ground black pepper

Fresh cilantro sprigs for garnish

# Chipotle Fried Onion Rings

*These addictive, spicy onion rings show how versatile* recados *can be. Make sure you slice the onions paper-thin. These are great as a snack.*

**Serves 2 to 4.**

Preheat oil in a deep fryer to 375°F. Mix together flour and Chipotle Rub in a large bowl until well blended. Add onion rings to flour mixture and toss well until evenly coated. Working in small batches, fry onions until crisp. Drain on paper towels and keep hot in a 250°F oven until serving.

# Summer Tomato, Avocado, and Chile Salad

*Some combinations are just perfect, like the flavors of garden-ripe tomato, avocado, sweet onion, and jalapeño. A splash of lime-and-garlic vinaigrette rounds out the flavors. Serve a big bowl of this salad alongside your favorite grill entrée, especially chicken and fish. Mix different colors of tomatoes, if available. And use your very best olive oil.*

**Serves 4 to 6.**

In a small, nonreactive bowl, whisk together jalapeño, lime juice, oil, ⅛ teaspoon salt, and garlic. In a large serving bowl, toss vinaigrette with tomatoes and onion until well coated. Add the avocados and toss gently. Season generously with salt and pepper. Garnish with cilantro sprigs and serve.

## Grilled Goat Cheese in Banana Leaves

2 pieces banana leaf, about 12 inches square each

1 poblano chile, roasted, peeled, seeded, deveined, and cut into ½-by-1½-inch strips

4 fresh epazote leaves (optional)

½ pound fresh soft goat cheese, formed into 2 disks each about ½ inch thick

2 teaspoons olive oil

Charred Tomato Mint Salsa (page 37)

*The wonderful thing about cooking in leaves is that they not only impart a delicious flavor, but also make for a dramatically beautiful presentation. Grilled soft goat cheese benefits from the subtle flavor that banana leaf imparts.*

**Serves 4.**

Light the grill and let burn down to a medium fire. Wash the banana leaves in hot water. Divide chile strips between banana leaves. Top each with 2 epazote leaves and a cheese disk. Drizzle each disk with olive oil. Fold leaves over cheese to wrap tightly like a package. Grill until leaves char slightly and cheese is very soft, about 5 minutes. Serve with salsa.

## Grilled Corn on the Cob with Chipotle Rub and Lime

4 ears of corn

1 tablespoon olive oil

About 1 tablespoon Chipotle Rub (page 31)

Lime wedges

Unsalted butter (optional)

*Nothing is better than sweet corn on the cob in season. Grilling corn adds a nutty, smoky flavor, as the sugar in the corn caramelizes over the fire. In the United States, people usually eat corn with butter. On street corners in Mexico, people eat roasted or boiled ears of corn with a sprinkling of ground red chile and a squeeze of lime juice. I love this combination using Chipotle Rub, with or without the butter.*

**Serves 1 to 4, depending on how good your corn is.**

Light the grill and let burn down to a medium-hot fire. If you have very sweet, fresh corn, go ahead and husk it. If your corn is more mature or out of season, it needs to be tenderized. Lay the unhusked ears over the fire and turn until the outside of the ears have turned brown and charred. Let corn rest, off heat, 10 minutes, then proceed with the recipe.

Husk the corn and brush lightly with olive oil. Grill over a medium-hot fire, turning frequently, until golden brown and lightly charred all over, about 6 minutes. Remove from the fire and sprinkle with Chipotle Rub to taste. Season with a squeeze of lime and, if you like, a little butter. Roll up your sleeves and enjoy.

# Grilled Nopales with Pumpkin Seed Salsa

*The dark green, flat "leaf" or paddle of the nopal cactus is widely eaten in Mexico. While it is a pain to clean, it has the advantage of being very simple to cook, and it is particularly delicious when grilled. Serve as described here, or chop coarsely, pile into warm tortillas, and top with the salsa.*

**Serves 4.**

Light the grill and let burn down to a medium fire. Brush the nopales with olive oil and season generously with salt and pepper. Grill until soft and browned, about 10 minutes. Serve as a side dish with the salsa.

**4 small nopales, each about 6 by 4 inches, spines removed**

**About 2 tablespoons olive oil**

**Salt and freshly ground black pepper to taste**

**Pumpkin Seed Salsa (page 42)**

# Grilled Wild Mushrooms

*To some people's apparent surprise, wild mushrooms are plentiful in the forested regions of Mexico, particularly after the rainy season. This dish makes an excellent vegetarian main course, either by itself or mixed with cooked black beans as a filling for tacos, enchiladas, or quesadillas.*

**Serves 4.**

If the mushrooms are gritty, wash them. Light the grill. Place a large cast-iron skillet or griddle on the grill over a very hot fire to preheat. Toss mushrooms with Garlic Rub. Pour oil on pan and add mushrooms. Sauté quickly until mushrooms begin to brown and pan is dry, about 5 minutes. Add the onion, chile, and, if using, epazote. Sauté briefly, about 1 minute. Remove from the heat, pour into a warm serving bowl, and serve immediately.

**¾ pound fresh morels, halved, or other flavorful mushrooms such as porcini, chanterelle, or shiitake, quartered**

**1 tablespoon Garlic Rub (page 29)**

**1 tablespoon olive oil**

**1 small white onion, minced**

**½ jalapeño chile or serrano chile with seeds, minced**

**6 fresh epazote leaves, chopped (optional)**

# Rice with Mint

2 tablespoons corn oil

1 cup converted rice

½ cup minced white onion

1½ cups water

1 teaspoon salt

6 fresh mint leaves, minced

*Hierba buena, or "mint," is widely used in Mexico as a savory seasoning. Unfortunately, in the United States, we are most familiar with mint as the favorite flavoring agent of toothpaste and mouthwash. If that hasn't spoiled your taste for the herb, try this unusual and delightful white rice. Cooking the mint in this way gentles its flavor. The frying of the rice is traditional. You must include this step in order to ensure an authentic flavor and texture.*

**Serves 4.**

Heat the oil in a saucepan over high heat until hot but not smoking. Add the onion and sauté until golden, about 5 minutes. Add the rice, lower heat to medium, and sauté until golden and beginning to brown, about 2 minutes. Add the water, salt, and mint and bring to a boil. Cover, reduce heat to low, and simmer exactly 14 minutes. Use a timer. Serve immediately or keep warm until needed.

# Drunken Beans

½ pound bacon, diced

1 large white onion, chopped

1 tablespoon dried Mexican oregano

1 clove garlic, chopped

2 cups dried pinto beans, picked over and soaked in cold water for 4 hours or overnight, then drained

6 cups water

½ cup sliced pickled jalapeño chiles

1 bottle (12 ounces) dark Mexican beer such as Negra Modelo

2½ teaspoons salt

*These beans are the sort you are likely to see throughout Mexico. Smoky bacon and bitter beer make them an excellent accompaniment to almost any Mexican meal. The beans should be whole, perfectly tender, and swimming in a generous amount of broth. Serve in a bowl with a spoon and enjoy their fragrance.*

**Serves 4 to 6.**

Preheat oven to 300°F. Place a large, ovenproof sauté pan over high heat. Add the bacon, onions, oregano, and garlic and sauté until lightly browned, about 10 minutes. Stir well as onions cook, scraping browned bits from bottom of pan. Add the beans, water, chiles, and beer, then bring to a boil, cover tightly, and put in the oven. Cook until soft, about 2 hours. Add more water if the beans begin to dry out. You should end up with a soupy bean stew, with the beans very soft but not falling apart.

Add 2 teaspoons salt, return beans to oven for 10 minutes, then check again for salt, adding remaining ½ teaspoon, if necessary. Serve immediately, or let cool, cover, and refrigerate until needed. Reheat over low heat, stirring frequently.

Drunken beans in a pot, with grilled chicken.

## Oaxacan-Style Black Beans with Avocado Leaves

**4 avocado leaves**

**2 cups dried black beans, picked over**

**1½ quarts water**

**1 small white onion, thickly sliced, pan-roasted until brown and soft**

**4 cloves garlic, pan-roasted until brown and soft, then peeled**

**¾ teaspoon salt**

*These are the best black beans there are. The fragrance of the avocado leaves is exotic, transporting you to a pre-Hispanic Mexico. Once the beans are cooked and puréed, they should be very loose, soft, and perfectly smooth. If you add a little more water and some crumbled, fried pasilla chiles, the beans make a perfect soup. These beans can also be baked in a 300°F oven for about 2 hours.*

**Serves 4 to 6.**

Put the avocado leaves in a dry skillet over medium heat and toast until browned and fragrant, about 10 seconds. Combine the avocado leaves, beans, water, onion, and garlic in a large pot and bring to a boil over high heat. Lower heat to a simmer, cover, and cook until very soft, about 1½ hours, adding more water as needed if beans begin to dry.

Drain cooked beans, reserving cooking liquid. Working in batches, purée beans in a blender until smooth, adding just enough cooking liquid to allow them to blend. Return to a saucepan and stir in salt. The mixture should be thick yet pourable. Reheat gently and serve immediately.

# Refried Black Beans with Plantains

*The best versions of these beans I have had are made with the crusty bits of pork and pork fat left in the bottom of the pot when carnitas are made. Yes, I know fried pork and lard are verboten, but oh, boy, are they good. These mashed, fried beans are served with strips of fried ripe plantain on top. Look, don't eat this way every day, but eat this way sometimes!*

**Serves 4 to 6.**

Put the beans, water, onion, and garlic in a large pot and bring to a boil. Lower heat to a simmer, cover, and cook until very soft, about 1½ hours, adding more water as needed if beans begin to dry. Drain off and reserve about half of the cooking liquid. Working in batches, purée beans in a blender with their remaining cooking liquid. You should have a very thick but pourable paste. Add some of the reserved cooking liquid, if necessary.

Melt lard in a large nonstick skillet over medium-high heat and add bean purée. Season with salt and, if using, add epazote leaves. Fry beans, stirring often, until brown and crusty, about 30 minutes. Timing will depend on looseness of your purée. Lower heat if the beans spatter too much. As a crust forms on the side of pan, scrape it back into the bean mixture. These crusty bits add flavor. Taste for seasoning.

When mixture is very dry, scrape beans into a bowl and return pan to medium-high heat. Add corn oil (or lard). Cut plantain in half crosswise, then cut each half in 3 lengthwise pieces. Fry plantains in oil until crisp and brown on both sides, about 3 minutes. In a small bowl, mix sour cream and heavy cream, if using. Garnish beans with plantains and sour cream mixture.

**2 cups dried black beans, picked over**

**6 cups water**

**1 small white onion, thickly sliced, pan-roasted until brown and soft**

**4 cloves garlic, pan-roasted until brown and soft, then peeled**

**⅓ cup pork lard, preferably freshly made, or ¼ cup packaged lard plus 1⅓ tablespoons bacon drippings or olive oil**

**1½ teaspoon salt**

**4 fresh epazote leaves (optional)**

**2 tablespoons corn oil or lard**

**1 ripe (black) plantain**

**1 tablespoon sour cream (optional)**

**1 tablespoon heavy cream (optional)**

# Black Beans with Nopales

1 small white onion, thickly sliced, pan-roasted until brown and soft

4 cloves garlic, pan-roasted until brown and soft, then peeled

1 tomato, pan-roasted until blistered, deeply browned and soft

2 cups dried black beans, picked over

6 cups water

1 tablespoon corn oil

2 chipotle chiles

2 teaspoons salt

2 cups cut-up nopales (½ by 1½ inches)

14 to 16 fresh epazote leaves

*This is Mexican country cooking at its best—subtle, intriguing, and very healthful. These beans make a great soup course or are wonderful as a side dish. Try adding Grilled Wild Mushrooms (page 103) and using the mixture as a taco or enchilada filling. In Oaxaca, these beans are eaten for breakfast with those giant toasted tortillas called* tlayudas.

**Serves 4 to 6.**

In a blender, purée the onion, garlic, and tomato until smooth. Put the beans, onion mixture, and water in a large pot. Bring to a boil, lower heat, cover, and simmer until just soft, about 1½ hours. Heat oil in a small skillet over medium-high heat. Add the chiles and fry until puffed and brown, about 10 seconds. Shake off excess oil and add to beans with salt, nopales, and 10 of the epazote leaves. Continue to cook until beans are very tender, about 30 minutes.

The beans should be very brothy, almost souplike. Remove the chipotles. If you want the beans to taste hotter, break up the chipotles and stir them back into the beans; otherwise, discard them. Serve beans in bowls with an epazote leaf in each as garnish.

# Rajas with Cream

*These are a little sinful but very wonderful. Strips of grilled peppers and onions are simmered together with sour cream and queso fresco. They make a great side dish or taco filling. If you cannot find queso fresco, feta can be used in its place; however, it has a different flavor. Try to track down the real thing.*

**Serves 4.**

Light the grill and let burn down to a medium-hot fire. Lightly brush the onion with oil and season on both sides with salt and pepper. Grill onion, chiles, and bell peppers until soft. Peel, seed, and devein the chiles and peppers, then cut into long strips.

   Put the oregano, sour cream, garlic, cheese, and salt in a blender or food processor and purée to a smooth paste. Pour into a medium-sized saucepan, add onions and chiles, and heat gently a few minutes to blend flavors.

**1 medium-sized white onion, thickly sliced**

**1 tablespoon olive oil**

**Salt and freshly ground black pepper to taste**

**4 poblano chiles**

**1 jalapeño chile (optional)**

**2 red bell peppers**

**¼ teaspoon dried Mexican oregano, toasted**

**½ cup sour cream**

**1 clove garlic, pan-roasted until brown and soft, then peeled**

**½ cup crumbled queso fresco**

**Pinch of salt**

# fiesta
# dishes

# It is impossible

to know Mexican food without understanding the importance of the fiesta. From the poorest of villages to the wealthiest of homes, elaborate fiestas celebrate saints' days, weddings, national holidays, and other significant dates. On a smaller scale, friends and family get together in large groups with great frequency to celebrate life.

These fiestas invariably revolve around elaborate traditional dishes. Tamales, moles, and some of the wonders of the Mexican grill—*barbacoa, cochinita pibil,* and *mixiotes.* In this chapter I give approximate recipes for six fiesta dishes. Some of these recipes are impossible to give exactly—quantities are large and techniques are imprecise. But don't be discouraged. Invite fifteen of your closest friends and dig a hole in the backyard. Have your own fiesta. Remember: Cooking is about love and sharing. Be generous in your heart.

# Fiesta Tacos: Mixed Grill with Assorted Salsas

*On fiesta days in Mexico, much of the celebratory fare is cooked on the streets by local families who set up stands and sell their specialties. Tacos are featured prominently, with fillings that showcase the regional foods. Often tacos are prepared on a special* comal *or griddle that looks something like a large, upside-down metal hat. Tortillas are heated next to frying meat over a little charcoal fire.*

*Prepare your favorite salsas and vegetable dishes ahead of time, and season meats and fish with* recados *for an easy backyard feast. Cooked meats can be coarsely chopped and kept warm at the edge of the fire in metal or ceramic bowls. Eat standing or sitting, with a little salsa music playing, perhaps a few people dancing, drinking toasts, singing, and children laughing and running—a fiesta. Have fun!*

**Serves 12 to 16.**

A few hours before serving or the day before, marinate meats and squid and prepare all salsas except Authentic Guacamole. Refrigerate everything. Prepare beans and rajas.

One hour before eating, light the grill. Reheat beans and rajas and keep warm. Bring salsas to room temperature. Grill chicken first, as it takes the longest. When chicken is done, place in a heatproof bowl and keep warm (to the side of the grill or in a 150°F oven). Grill beef and squid. Place separately in heatproof bowls and keep warm along with chicken. Grill corn. Make the guacamole. Heat the tortillas, 1 or 2 at a time, directly on the grill, and chop meats. Arrange all the food on a table outdoors for your guests, and serve tortillas first, then meat, seafood, and poultry, followed by salsas, beans, rajas, and garnishes. Let your guests serve themselves, building their own tacos.

**2 recipes Spiced Skirt Steak Fajitas, meat only (page 94)**

**2 recipes Chicken in a Molcajete, meat only (page 74)**

**2 recipes Grilled Squid Yucatán Style, seafood only (page 64)**

**2 recipes Pico de Gallo (page 41)**

**2 recipes Charred Habanero Salsa (page 39)**

**2 recipes Pumpkin Seed Salsa (page 42)**

**4 recipes Authentic Guacamole (page 43)**

**3 recipes Drunken Beans (page 104)**

**4 recipes Rajas with Cream (page 109)**

**4 recipes Grilled Corn on the Cob with Chipotle Rub and Lime (page 102)**

**Small tortillas**

**Lime wedges, fresh cilantro leaves, and diced radish for garnish**

# Grilled Seafood Stew in Fresh Coconuts

2 large green (fresh) coconuts, heavy for their size and sloshing with liquid

1 medium white onion, chopped

1 clove garlic, minced

1 poblano chile, seeded, deveined, and diced into 1-inch pieces

½ cup diced fresh pineapple

¼ pound peeled and deveined shrimp

¼ pound cleaned squid

¼ pound snapper or grouper fillet, cut into 1-inch-wide strips

1 habanero chile, with seeds, cut into rings

2 fresh epazote leaves, chopped

2 roasted tomatoes, chopped

1 teaspoon achiote recado

Salt to taste

2 tablespoons coarsely chopped fresh cilantro

Lime wedges

*For me, food involves a high degree of fantasy. This dish is one that I have tried to find on the west coast of Mexico. I have talked to people who have had dishes like this and it certainly makes sense to cook a seafood stew in that beachside bowl, the coconut. But I had never eaten it until I made it for this book.*

*What I love is the gentle smokiness of the coconut against the more assertive flavor of the chile-infused stew. Buy a few extra coconuts when you make this dish. Chill them, cut off the tops, pour out the juice into a shaker glass, add a little sugar, a good measure of dark rum (Havana Club is my favorite, although, like Cuban cigars, it is not available in the United States), a squeeze of lime, and some ice. Shake well and strain back into the coconut. Take two long straws, a big comfortable hammock, a sunny day, a deserted beach, a beautiful person whom you love, and, well, you get the idea. Salud!*

**Serves 2.**

Light the grill and let burn down to a medium fire. With a sturdy, short-bladed knife, cut the tops off the coconuts. Reserve lids if they are not too broken. Strain the coconut liquid into a bowl and set aside. If the coconuts do not stand up on their own, cut another slice off the bottom so they do. In a bowl, mix together all the remaining ingredients except the cilantro and lime wedges.

Divide the mixture between the coconuts. Pour in reserved coconut juice to fill to top and replace lids or cover with foil. Set over the fire, cover grill, and cook until seafood is cooked through, about 15 minutes. Remove the lids, stir in cilantro, and serve with lime wedges.

## Skewered Baby Goat or Lamb

1 kid or suckling lamb (12 to 15 pounds or more), split almost in half from chest to tail and pushed down on a flat surface so that it lays flat in one piece

½ cup Chipotle Rub (page 31)

Basting Sauce (recipe follows)

Norteño-Style Árbol Chile Salsa (page 38)

Authentic Guacamole (page 43)

Diced radish for garnish

*Throughout south Texas and northern Mexico (an area that all used to belong to Mexico) the great delicacy is* cabrito, *or kid (suckling goat), one of the world's great meats and one that is equally loved by Greeks and Italians. But I have eaten no better kid than in the area around Nuevo Laredo, Mexico.*

*A large, shallow fire is built, much like the one for Cowboy-Style Rib of Beef (page 118). The kid, typically weighing 12 to 15 pounds, is split and skewered on metal rods angled over the fire. The seasoned meat is basted and cooked until the outside is crispy and the flesh is tender and moist. A single kid serves no more than 6 people. Serve with Drunken Beans (page 104) and, of course, plenty of fresh, hot tortillas. If* cabrito *is unavailable, you can substitute baby lamb.*

**Serves 6.**

One hour before you want to cook the goat or lamb, rub it generously all over with Chipolte Rub. Build a large mesquite wood fire on the ground inside a ring of rocks. Skewer the kid or lamb on a metal rod (a rebar used in construction is perfect for this). When the fire burns down to some good coals, hammer the rod into the ground just at the edge of the fire. Prop it up with rocks around the base and angle the rod so it leans out over the fire at a 60-degree angle. Alternatively, rig a spit across the top of the fire.

Brush the kid or lamb with the basting sauce every 10 to 15 minutes and keep the fire very hot, but do not let flames touch the meat. Turn the meat every 15 minutes and cook until it registers 130°F on a meat thermometer. This should take about 1½ hours. When done, carve portions directly off the kid or lamb on its stake. Garnish with diced radish and serve with salsa and guacamole.

2 bottles (12 ounces each) dark Mexican beer such as Negra Modelo or Dos Equis

1 cup freshly squeezed lime juice

1 pound (4 sticks) unsalted butter

2 medium-sized white onions, coarsely chopped

**Basting Sauce:** Combine all the ingredients in a medium-sized, nonreactive saucepan and heat to melt the butter. Keep warm next to the fire.

**Makes about 7 cups.**

# Leg of Lamb in Maguey Cactus Leaves

*There is a restaurant on Insurgentes Sur, south of Mexico City in Tlalpan, called El Arroyo. Arroyo will feed three thousand people on a busy Sunday—seemingly, all at one time. They sell so much of this dish there that they raise their own lambs on a ranch north of Mexico City. At the restaurant, the dish is cooked in huge, specially constructed stone pits. The lamb is stood upright against the side walls of the preheated pits, and the pit is covered first with sheets of metal and then with dirt. Hours later, the lamb emerges succulent, meltingly tender, and ready to eat with tortillas and salsa* borracho—*a special salsa made from* pulque *(the fermented milk of the same cactus used to make tequila), pasilla chiles, and crumbled cheese. That particular salsa cannot be made in the United States because we cannot get* pulque. *Instead, I have given you a recipe for another salsa based on pasilla chiles. Near San Francisco, where I live, and throughout the Southwest, maguey cactus (century plant) is a fairly common ornamental plant. If you can't find maguey, you could use banana leaves, although the flavor is quite different. Serve with double recipes of Soledad's Salsa (page 46), Authentic Guacamole (page 43), Drunken Beans (page 104), and plenty of fresh, hot tortillas.*

**Serves 8 to 10.**

One day before you cook the lamb, cut 10 deep slashes in the meat. Push a mint leaf and a sliver of onion into each of the slashes. Rub the meat all over with Garlic Rub. Put the leg of lamb in a large, food storage bag and pour in beer. Seal bag and refrigerate until ready to use. (Lamb is best used the next day. Do not marinate longer than 2 days. Meat will get saltier and drier with time.)

Light the grill or water smoker and let burn down to a slow fire. Scald the maguey leaf with hot water, then hold over an open flame until it blisters slightly. Put the lamb in the center of the inside (curved) part of the leaf and fold the leaf over to cover the lamb partially. Tie with heavy cotton twine. If using banana leaf, wash in hot water, then lay meat in center of crossed leaves and wrap as neatly as possible into a package. Tie with string.

Cook lamb in covered grill or water smoker, keeping a very slow but steady fire (about 250°F), until fork tender, 6 to 8 hours. Add charcoal as necessary to maintain heat. Cut lamb into small chunks and serve on a warm platter topped with chopped white onion and radish.

**1 leg of lamb, aitchbone removed and trimmed of some fat (6 to 8 pounds)**

**¼ cup Garlic Rub (page 29)**

**10 fresh mint leaves**

**1 small white onion, cut into slivers**

**1 bottle (12 ounces) dark Mexican beer such as Negra Modelo**

**1 maguey cactus leaf, about 5 feet long, spines removed, or 2 pieces banana leaf, 12 by 24 inches each**

**Coarsely chopped white onion and diced radish for garnish**

# Cowboy-Style Rib of Beef

1 rib of beef (at least 2 ribs in one piece weighing 3 pounds, up to 7 ribs weighing about 20 pounds), trimmed of all but ¼ inch fat

Chipotle Rub (page 31)

Wild sage sprigs or rosemary sprigs (optional)

Basting Sauce (recipe follows)

*South Texas and adjacent northern Mexico is cattle country. All of it used to belong to Mexico, and the food is similar on both sides of the border. The natives have long cooked meat over mesquite fires. The Spaniards brought iron for grills and cattle to grill on them. When the legendary cowman, Charlie Goodnight, was asked on his ninetieth birthday to what he attributed his longevity and fitness, he replied, "I eat beef three times a day with plenty of taller [fat]." You start with a prime rib of beef, add some seasoning, a spit or a long stake, a mesquite fire, and a few trimmings. This is food to be eaten out of one's hand while standing, talking, and drinking. Plenty of cold beer before dinner, and lots of tequila combined with some Tejano music afterward—all this makes for a memorable party. Serve Green Chile Salsa (page 39) or Norteño-Style Árbol Chile Salsa (page 38), Drunken Beans (page 104), sliced onions and avocados, diced radish, and lots of hot flour tortillas.*

**Serves 4 to 20.**

One day before the barbecue, generously rub Chipotle Rub all over the beef. Six hours before serving, build a large mesquite fire on the ground inside a ring of rocks or in a large grill fitted with a rotisserie. Skewer the beef on the spit or stake and suspend about 3 feet above a hot fire. Using a brush, or, if desired, a sprig of sage or rosemary, baste the beef well with the sauce and continue to baste every 10 to 20 minutes. Keep the fire hot, but not flaming very high. Rotate beef every 15 minutes and cook until it registers 130°F on a meat thermometer for medium-rare, about 1½ hours for a 3-pound roast, and the same for a 20-pound roast.

Let roast rest on a large cutting board 15 minutes before carving.

1 cup Norteño-Style Árbol Chile Salsa (page 38)

2 bottles (12 ounces) Mexican beer such as Bohemia

1 pound (4 sticks) unsalted butter

2 medium-sized white onions, chopped

**Basting Sauce:** *This sauce keeps the meat moist while imparting a rich, spicy flavor to the surface of the meat.*

**Makes about 7 cups, enough for 10 pounds of beef.**

Heat all the ingredients together in a medium-sized, nonreactive saucepan and keep warm next to the fire.

# Leg of Venison in Clay

*One of the most primitive methods of cooking involves wrapping foods in mud or clay and cooking in a pit. When properly done, the joint of meat can be presented in its clay shell and the shell dramatically cracked at the table. I think the rich, slightly gamy flavor of venison is amplified by the hermetic seal of the clay. When leaves of hierba santa are added as a seasoning, the resulting dish is a haunting reminder of the exotic and sophisticated flavors of pre-Hispanic cookery. You may cook this in a conventional oven at 250°F, but when done on a grill the smokiness will permeate the clay and add another dimension to the dish. Serve with Pumpkin Seed Salsa (page 42), Black Beans with Nopales (page 108), and plenty of fresh, hot tortillas. If venison is unavailable, substitute a leg of lamb.*

**Serves 8 to 10.**

1 leg of venison (6 to 8 pounds)

1 tablespoon kosher salt

1½ cups Adobo Recado (page 33)

1 piece burlap or other heavy cotton fabric, about 3 feet square

10 pounds potter's clay

6 to 8 fresh *hierba santa* leaves

Coarsely chopped white onion and fresh cilantro leaves for garnish

One hour before cooking, rub the venison with the salt and *recado*. Lay the burlap out on a clean, level surface. Press the clay into a round 30 inches in diameter on the center of the burlap. Arrange half the *hierba santa* leaves in the center of the clay and lay meat on top. Place remaining *hierba santa* leaves on the meat. Using the cloth to help you, lift edges of clay and fold over the meat. Completely cover meat with the clay, pressing edges together to seal. Don't worry if the clay cracks; just push it back together as if it were pastry. Try to form the clay package into the shape of the leg as you wrap it. When the leg is completely covered with clay, wrap the clay in the burlap, drawing the fabric tight; this helps prevent the clay from cracking.

Light the grill and let burn down to a slow fire. Cook the wrapped meat in the covered grill, keeping a very slow but steady fire (about 250°F), until meat is done, 4 to 5 hours. There is no way to check the meat other than to listen for sounds of boiling juices or to look for steam escaping. If you see juices boiling out of the clay, the meat is done. Be very careful handling the clay; it will retain heat a long time.

After the meat is done, remove the burlap if it has not baked into the clay. Let meat rest in clay 30 minutes, then present meat in the clay at the table. Crack open clay with a hammer, discard the *hierba santa*, and transfer the meat to a serving platter. Cut meat into small chunks and serve topped with the onion and cilantro.

# desserts

# After a meal

of grilled, spicy foods, I like to eat a little something sweet. But I don't like to go to a lot of fuss when I'm grilling

outside. I suggest one of the following six desserts. They are easy to make and terrific for cleansing the palate

after spicy food. If you have never grilled fruit, please try it. I think you will be pleasantly surprised by the ease

of making a sophisticated dessert from simple ingredients.

# Grilled Bananas with Rum Ice Cream

*Almost any fruit benefits from being gently grilled until it is warm and browned on the outside. And what better accompaniment to warm, grilled fruit than ice cream, particularly a delicious rum ice cream? This dessert is easy to finish after you have grilled your main course.*

**Serves 4.**

Light the grill and let burn down to a slow fire. In a medium-sized bowl, carefully toss the bananas with the butter and sugar. Grill until brown on the outside and cooked through, about 3 minutes. Since the bananas are fragile, you may want to grill them on one side only. Serve like a banana split with rum ice cream and hot chocolate sauce or warm cajeta.

**Rum Ice Cream:** *The better the rum, the better this ice cream tastes.*

**Makes about 1½ quarts.**

Place the cream and milk in a medium-sized, heavy saucepan. Scrape seeds from vanilla bean into cream mixture, then drop in bean as well. Add lemon zest and bring just to a boil. In a large mixing bowl, whisk together sugar and egg yolks until well blended. Slowly add the scalded cream mixture, whisking vigorously all the while. Return mixture to saucepan, place over medium-low heat, and cook, stirring constantly, until mixture thickens and coats the back of a spoon, about 8 minutes. Do not let it boil.

Strain into a bowl and let cool. Stir in rum, cover, and chill until cold. Freeze in an ice cream maker according to the manufacturer's instructions.

4 ripe bananas, peeled and split in half lengthwise

4 tablespoons (½ stick) unsalted butter, melted

¼ cup firmly packed brown sugar

Rum Ice Cream (recipe follows)

Mexican Hot Chocolate Sauce (page 126) or warm cajeta (page 126)

2 cups heavy cream

2 cups milk

1 vanilla bean, split in half lengthwise

1 piece lemon zest, about ½ by 2 inches

⅔ cup firmly packed brown sugar

8 egg yolks

¼ cup good-quality dark rum such as Bacardi Black

# Grilled Tropical Fruits in Banana Leaves

1 ripe mango, peeled and cut into wedges

1 cup pineapple chunks

2 ripe bananas, peeled and cut into chunks

4 guavas or feijoas, carefully peeled and cut into chunks

2 passion fruits, pulp scooped out

4 pieces banana leaf, about 12 inches square each

Juice of 2 limes

4 fresh mint leaves

2 tablespoons firmly packed brown sugar

2 tablespoons unsalted butter

Rum Ice Cream (optional, page 123)

*These aromatic packages are fun to serve for dessert after a spicy meal. They are delectable by themselves, or would certainly benefit from a scoop of ice cream. If you can't find all of the fruits listed here, don't despair. Just cook with what is available.*

**Serves 4.**

Light the grill. In a bowl, mix together the mango, pineapple, bananas, guavas or feijoas, and passion fruits. Wash banana leaves well in hot water. Lay banana leaves on countertop and divide fruit mixture evenly among them. Sprinkle each with lime juice, add a mint leaf, and dot each with ½ tablespoon each butter and sugar. Wrap leaves around fruit to form a package. Rewrap in heavy-duty aluminum foil.

Grill over a hot fire until bubbling hot, about 8 minutes. Let guests unwrap their own package. If you wish, serve with ice cream.

# Grilled Figs with Honey and Queso Fresco Tart

*Just wait until you try fresh figs, warm from the grill. The very simple and delicious tart makes a splendid foil for the wonderful rich flavor of the figs. The tart filling is best made with the slightly sour queso fresco, but can also be made with ricotta or even a fresh goat cheese.*

**Serves 8.**

**For the pastry:** Preheat oven to 375°F. Measure the 1½ cups flour into a mixing bowl. Add the butter and, using a pastry blender or 2 knives, cut into flour until mixture resembles coarse meal. Working quickly, add water, 1 tablespoon at a time, just until mixture holds together. Gather into a ball, flatten into a disk, wrap in waxed paper, refrigerate, and let rest in the refrigerator for 1 hour to 2 days. (Dough can also be frozen for up to 2 months.)

When ready to bake, roll out dough on a lightly floured board into a round ⅛ inch thick and fit into a 10-inch tart pan. Prick bottom of dough about 10 times with tines of a fork, line with aluminum foil or waxed paper, and weight down with pie weights or dried beans. Bake until lightly browned, about 15 minutes. Remove weights or beans and foil or paper and bake another 5 minutes until fully baked and golden brown all over.

**For the filling:** Preheat oven to 375°F. In a medium-sized bowl, whisk eggs and flour together until evenly blended. Add the cheese, sugar, and orange-flower water and mix well. Pour into the prebaked pie shell and bake until custard is set and lightly browned, about 35 minutes. If edges of pastry threaten to get too dark, cover with pieces of aluminum foil. Let cool to room temperature before serving.

**For the figs:** Light the grill and let burn down to a slow fire. Melt the honey and butter together in a small saucepan, over the grill if convenient, and if not, over low heat. In a small bowl, toss figs with half of the butter mixture. Grill figs until brown and bubbling slightly, about 3 minutes. Put cooked figs in a small serving bowl and pour remaining butter mixture over them. Serve warm with the tart.

**Pastry**
1½ cups all-purpose flour, plus more for dusting work surface

8 tablespoons (½ stick) cold unsalted butter, cut into small bits

Pinch of salt

4 to 5 tablespoons ice water

**Tart Filling**
4 eggs

1 tablespoon all-purpose flour

1 pound queso fresco, ricotta, or very fresh goat cheese

⅔ cup sugar

1 teaspoon orange-flower water

**Figs**
⅓ cup honey

4 tablespoons (½ stick) unsalted butter

12 fresh figs, cut in half

## Ice Cream Sundaes with Mexican Hot Chocolate and Warm Cajeta Sauce

2 jars (8 ounces each) cajeta (optional)

1 quart vanilla ice cream, or preferred flavor

Mexican Hot Chocolate Sauce (optional; recipe follows)

Cajeta Cream (next page)

*I love hot fudge sundaes. This sundae is both easy to make and absolutely sinful. If I picked one dessert from this book that would please the most people with the least work, this is it. Most of the ingredients are readily available and require almost no preparation.*

**Serves 8.**

If using, place jars of cajeta in a saucepan of hot water and warm over medium heat. Keep warm until needed.

When ready for dessert, scoop ice cream into cold sundae glasses or bowls. Pour a generous amount of warm chocolate sauce or cajeta, or both, over each serving. Top with cajeta cream and serve with an iced tea spoon.

½ pound Mexican chocolate, chopped

2 cups half-and-half

**Mexican Hot Chocolate Sauce:** *Mexican chocolate has its own particular dark flavor. Use any brand you prefer, but do use Mexican chocolate, or you will miss the special connection to the country.*

**Makes about 2¼ cups.**

Heat chocolate and half-and-half in a saucepan over low heat, stirring often, until chocolate is melted. Keep warm until needed.

# Cajeta Flan

*This flan always gets raves. It is easy to prepare ahead of time, which makes it the perfect party dessert. When you top the flan with the Cajeta Cream and crushed almond praline, it becomes an elegant caramel treat. Cajeta is a blend of goat's milk and sugar cooked together for a long time until the whole reduces and caramelizes. It is easily found in jars in Mexican and Latin American markets.*

**Serves 6.**

1 cup cajeta

5 egg yolks

3 whole eggs

2 cups half-and-half

½ cup sugar

2 tablespoons water

Chocolate Sauce (recipe follows)

2 to 3 tablespoons crushed almond or pecan praline (optional; see note)

Cajeta Cream (recipe follows)

Preheat oven to 300°F. In a large bowl, whisk together cajeta, egg yolks, whole eggs, and half-and-half until well blended. Set aside. Put the sugar and water in a small, heavy saucepan and place over medium-high heat. Swirl pan frequently until sugar dissolves and comes to a boil. Let boil without stirring until it turns a light nut brown. Immediately remove from the heat and pour into a 1½-quart mold. Swirl mold to coat bottom evenly with caramel.

Add the cajeta mixture to the mold and cover with aluminum foil. Put mold in a deep roasting pan and add hot water to come halfway up the sides of the mold. Bake until set, about 45 minutes. Let cool completely, then pour Chocolate Sauce over the top. Refrigerate until needed. The chocolate layer will harden.

When ready to serve, run a knife around the inside edge of the mold. Place a deep platter over the mold, then invert the platter and mold together. Lift off mold. Sprinkle with the praline, if using. Serve each portion with a generous dollop of Cajeta Cream.

**Note: Use your favorite recipe for almond or pecan praline (caramelized sugar with almonds or pecans) or finely crush purchased almond brittle in a food processor.**

**Chocolate Sauce:** Heat chocolate and half-and-half in a small saucepan over low heat, stirring often, until chocolate is melted. Keep warm until needed.

**Makes ½ cup.**

¼ pound Mexican chocolate, chopped

1 tablespoon half-and-half

**Cajeta Cream:** Cajeta gives whipped cream a rich caramel flavor. In a large mixing bowl, whip together the cream and cajeta until mixture stands in soft peaks. Refrigerate until needed.

**Makes 2 cups.**

¼ cup cajeta

1 cup heavy cream

# sources

The mainstreaming of Mexican food can be seen in supermarkets across the country. They nearly all have an ethnic section that includes a large number of Mexican and Latin American food products. The produce section carries fresh and dried chiles, fresh cilantro, and tomatillos in season.

Still, some ingredients can be harder to find, although most are no farther than your local Mexican or Latin American grocery. Farmers' markets are another excellent resource, especially for fresh and dried chiles. In addition, I have provided a list of some companies, including my own (Marimba Products at my restaurant, Café Marimba), that will happily mail-order ingredients.

**Marimba Products**
2317 Chestnut Street
San Francisco, CA 94123
Telephone: 415-347-0111
Fax: 415-347-3823
Catalog available.

We carry a full line of herbs and spices, including epazote, dried chiles, *hierba santa*, avocado leaves, and a wide range of prepared salsas, *recados*, and moles.

**Los Chileros de Nuevo Mexico**
P. O. Box 6215
Santa Fe, NM 87502
Telephone: 505-471-6967
Catalog available.

This company specializes in New Mexico food products and carries all types of dried chiles.

**It's About Thyme**
P. O. Box 878
Manchaca, TX 78652
Telephone: 512-280-1192
Catalog available.

An amazing array of herb plants that are shipped to customers via UPS. Buy *hierba santa* and epazote, both of which grow well in mild climates.

**La Palma**
2884 24th Street
San Francisco, CA 94110
Telephone: 415-647-1500
No catalog.

This is a terrific shop in the tradition of barrio markets across the United States. It is best to go in person and definitely worth the visit. They will ship, but are a bit reluctant to do so.

**Texas Wild Game Co-op**
P. O. Box 530
Ingram, TX 78025
Telephone: 512-367-5875
Catalog available.

When you want game and are not a hunter, call them for venison, antelope, wild boar, game sausages, and the all-time best bacon.

**Tierra Vegetables**
13684 Chalk Hill Road
Healdsburg, CA 95448
Telephone: 707-433-5666
Price list available.

This small farmer grows many chile varieties without the use of pesticides, herbicides, or fumigants.

# index

# table of equivalents

The exact equivalents in the following tables have been rounded forconvenience.

## Oven Temperatures

| F. | Celsius | Gas | F. | Celsius | Gas |
|----|---------|-----|-----|---------|-----|
| 250 | 120 | ½ | 400 | 200 | 6 |
| 275 | 140 | 1 | 425 | 220 | 7 |
| 300 | 150 | 2 | 450 | 230 | 8 |
| 325 | 160 | 3 | 475 | 240 | 9 |
| 350 | 180 | 4 | 500 | 260 | 10 |
| 375 | 190 | 5 | | | |

### US/UK

oz=ounce

lb=pound

in=inch

ft=foot

tbl=tablespoon

fl oz=fluid ounce

## Liquids

| US | Metric | UK | US | Metric | UK |
|----|--------|-----|-----|--------|-----|
| 2 tbl | 30 ml | 1 fl oz | ¾ cup | 180 ml | 6 fl oz |
| ¼ cup | 60 ml | 2 fl oz | 1 cup | 250 ml | 8 fl oz |
| ⅓ cup | 80 ml | 3 fl oz | 1½ cups | 375 ml | 12 fl oz |
| ½ cup | 125 ml | 4 fl oz | 2 cups | 500 ml | 16 fl oz |
| ⅔ cup | 160 ml | 5 fl oz | 4 cups/1 qt | 1 liter | 32 fl oz |

### Metric

g=gram

kg=kilogram

mm=millimeter

cm=centimeter

ml=milliliter

l=liter

## Length Measures

| US/UK | Metric | US/UK | Metric |
|-------|--------|-------|--------|
| ⅛ in | 3 mm | 6 in | 15 cm |
| ¼ in | 6 mm | 7 in | 18 cm |
| ½ in | 12 mm | 8 in | 20 cm |
| 1 in | 2.5 cm | 9 in | 23 cm |
| 2 in | 5 cm | 10 in | 25 cm |
| 3 in | 7.5 cm | 11 in | 28 cm |
| 4 in | 10 cm | 12 in/1 ft | 30 cm |
| 5 in | 13 cm | | |

## Weights

| US/UK | Metric | US/UK | Metric |
|-------|--------|-------|--------|
| 1 oz | 30 g | 10 oz | 315 g |
| 2 oz | 60 g | 12 oz (¾ lb) | 375 g |
| 3 oz | 90 g | 14 oz | 440 g |
| 4 oz (¼ lb) | 125 g | 16 oz (1 lb) | 500 g |
| 5 oz (⅓ lb) | 155 g | 1½ lb | 750 g |
| 6 oz | 185 g | 2 lb | 1 kg |
| 7 oz | 220 g | 3 lb | 1.5 kg |
| 8 oz (½ lb) | 250 g | | |